# A Professional's Guide to Older Adults' Life Review

# A Professional's Guide to Older Adults' Life Review

## Releasing the Peace Within

### JAMES J. MAGEE
*College of New Rochelle*

Lexington Books

*D.C. Heath and Company · Lexington, Massachusetts · Toronto*

*Library of Congress Cataloging-in-Publication Data*

Magee, James J.
   A professional's guide to older adults' life review releasing the peace within.

   Bibliography: p.
   Includes index.
      1. Aged—Psychology.    2. Reminiscing.    3. Psychology—Biographical methods.
   I. Title.
   BF724.85.R45M34   1988          155.67          88-45223
   ISBN 0-669-19413-1 (alk. paper)

Published simultaneously in Canada
Printed in the United States of America
International Standard Book Number: 0-669-19413-1
Library of Congress Catalog Card Number: 88-45223

The paper used in this publication meets the minimum requirements of American National Standard for Information Sciences—Permanence of Paper for Printed Library Materials, ANSI Z39.48-1984. ♾®™

88 89 90 91 92 8 7 6 5 4 3 2 1

*To* NANCY, *and our children,*
MARY CECILIA
JAMES
JOHN
KATE

# Contents

# Acknowledgments

I am indebted to the many people who taught me to listen with caring and attention to the reminiscences of older adults. My mother modeled these traits for me throughout the years she was the primary caregiver for her parents. In 1973, I enrolled in the postgraduate family therapy program at the Center for Family Learning, New Rochelle, New York. Under the tutelage of the director of the center, Dr. Philip Guerin, and my instructors, Monica McGoldrick, Peggy Papp, and Dr. Norman Ackerman, I drew upon the life review of the older members of my extended family to understand better my own makeup. In the process, I discovered how life review can heal troubling memories and affirm meaning and purpose in the lives of older adults.

I appreciate the support that so many people graciously gave to the development of this volume. My wife, Nancy, and Dr. Ronald Federico, my colleague in the Westchester Social Work Education Consortium, generously read multiple drafts of the text and made many valuable recommendations. The College of New Rochelle provided a grant to continue my research and a sabbatical leave for writing the manuscript.

I want to express my deepest gratitude to the many older adults who shared their life review with me. Their wisdom is the guide for what appears in these pages.

# Introduction

THIS book examines the contribution that life review makes in the lives of older adults. It explains the nature and functions of life review, and recommends steps that professionals in the human services can take to enhance the life review process. Examples of older adults' enriching their lives through life review appear throughout the book. (Actual names and details of events have been altered to ensure anonymity.) By integrating these examples with the findings of my own research and that of other gerontologists during the past fifteen years, this book describes how life review helps older adults make their lives more intelligible to themselves and those who care for them. It records how life review helps older adults find meaning and gratification in their personal history, even when sorrow and failure have formed significant parts of it. Finally, it shows how life review helps them find purpose and significance in the years ahead of them.

This book elaborates upon five guidelines professional caregivers can use to facilitate the life review of older adults. These guidelines encourage the reader to (1) approach life review as a natural, developmental process; (2) develop a family context for interpreting the content of life review; (3) involve confidants and other listeners in the review process; (4) draw upon poetic imagery in evoking life review; and (5) recognize how life review can be a spiritual experience for religiously committed older adults.

Chapter 1 defines life review and distinguishes it from the broader category of reminiscence. Though life review occurs throughout the life cycle, this chapter examines it as a resource that especially enriches the lives of older adults. Through its reconstruction of the past, life review can heal memories, promote self-acceptance, and diminish anxieties about dying.

Chapter 2 presents a family context for interpreting the themes that recur in a person's life review. This context refers to patterns of interaction among family members that have a cumulative impact upon the themes that will influence an individual's life course. By guiding the attention of older adults and their confidants to the significance of this impact, professional caregivers can help demystify the tenacity with which the same themes reappear in life review and lighten the severity with which reviewers may assess their past.

Chapter 3 looks at life review as an interactive experience between older people doing the reviewing and those who listen carefully to these memories. Older adults usually want to share the lessons and insights derived from their review. Some prefer to discuss their memories with a trusted friend or family member. Others may choose to participate in groups where members respond to one another's life review.

Confidants can be enriched from the life review process as much as the reviewers themselves. Younger listeners can find antecedents for their own behavior in the anecdotal history they hear. Kin can assess family strengths and liabilities. Staff in nursing homes can improve the social functioning of residents.

Chapter 4 describes how images from poetry facilitate life review. They prompt memory, capture the emotional tone of events they evoke, and compellingly portray the meaning the reviewer attributes to these events. Poetic images can involve older adults intellectually and emotionally, "packaging" memories so they feel more manageable for ongoing reflection. Discussion of imagery in favorite poems is also a catalyst for self-expression among members of groups discussing life review.

Chapter 5 considers life review as a spiritual experience. Because it raises questions about the meaning of life and measures behavior against deeply held values, life review can be approached as a profoundly religious experience, as well as a psychological one.

Professional caregivers can draw upon this guide to inaugurate programs of life review in community centers, parishes, congregate living arrangements, and nursing homes, and to participate constructively and enjoyably in the life review process of their clients. Students in nursing, social work, psychology, and gerontology can use it to deepen their understanding of life span development, life satisfaction, and family systems.

Following chapter 5 and organized chapter by chapter, there is a list of references for the sources cited. A comprehensive bibliography concerning reminiscence and life review follows the references.

# 1

# Life Review: Doing What Comes Naturally

## Introduction

This chapter explores the developmental, self-affirming nature of life review. It begins by discussing the functions of reminiscence in general, since life review is a form of reminiscence. It then elaborates upon the benefits of life review itself, especially its contribution to older adults in helping them protect their identity, cope with grief and personal loss, and maintain self-esteem. Finally, the chapter explains ways of decreasing the risk of depression that sometimes accompanies life review.

## Reminiscence

Discussion of the natural developmental character of life review should begin with an examination of reminiscence. Life review is a form of reminiscence, and an appreciation for the functions and dynamics of reminiscence enhances an understanding of life review as well. Because reminiscing generally becomes "second nature" after seven years of age, people lose sight of its subtle operation.

Reminiscence occurs when a person recalls long-forgotten incidents, dwells on them, and recaptures the emotions that originally accompanied them, often while trying to convey these felt experiences to a listener. These recollections are usually clear and vivid, accompanied by pleasant or uncomfortable emotions varying in intensity. They may focus upon any period of the life cycle and any aspect of a person's life.

Sometimes reminiscence occurs spontaneously when minor events, only at the edge of people's attention, evoke a train of freely associated recollections that lead them back into their past. On other occasions, people purposefully recall the past. They may do this to enhance self-understanding, provide entertainment, protect their self-esteem, cope with problems, or illustrate a lesson.

For example, let's begin with Janet. Janet was seventy years old, unmarried, and recently retired from her position as director of social services in a municipal hospital. She lived with her ninety-one-year-old mother who maintained an active daily routine of crocheting, correspondence, and household tasks. Just before Janet was to leave with a friend for two weeks in the Canadian Rockies, her mother fell and broke her right arm and leg. After she left the hospital, Janet's mother had to stay in a nursing home for three weeks, where she received physiotherapy. Janet's vacation coincided with the stay in the nursing home.

Because these weeks were the only time her friend was free to join her, Janet was disheartened at the prospect of postponing her vacation. As she pondered what to do, she recalled a scene from her adolescence that her mother had repeated many times. During that period, her mother prepared three dinners daily. The first she delivered to her frail widowed mother who lived three blocks away. The second was for Janet and herself. The third she served to her husband upon his return from work. Then, as she and Janet cleaned up, she would announce, "I'll get no credit for this! I resent every minute of it! An only child gets the full load!"

The reminiscence helped free Janet from her indecision. If she changed her plans, she knew she would hold it against her mother the entire time she tended to her during her recuperation. On the other hand, if she went on the vacation, she knew her mother would resent that she did not receive from Janet the attention that she had shown her own mother. Given the consequences of her options, Janet decided that she would be more comfortable "getting the grief" from her mother than from herself.

It is also commonplace to hear older adults purposefully use reminiscence to achieve "role parity" and "time parity" with younger people. In examples of "role parity," older adults "identify themselves with former occupational and social roles" that provide equal status or superiority vis-à-vis the person with whom they are interacting.[1]

A registered nurse, for instance, was completing his internship at a municipal senior center as a requirement for his graduate degree in gerontology. He was talking with several men preparing for a pool game about all that he had learned during the year from his experiences at the center. Eventually, one of the players interrupted him to regale the group with an account of his own trials as a psychologist beginning a practice in family therapy out of an office in his home. According to his story, a family rang the office bell at the very time he was haranguing his son about a lamentable report card. When the father said that they would continue the topic later, his son threatened to answer the door there and then and tell the family what a "lousy father" their therapist was. The tale was not only amusing, but also served to alert the intern that this "idle old man" was, in fact, also a seasoned mental health professional whose credentials exceeded those of the intern.

Reminiscence is also used to establish "time parity" with a younger associate. By "bringing the older person mentally back through time to the same age as that of the younger person," memories, in effect, erase the differences in age.[2] This can be seen with the grandfather who admonishes the child, "When I was your age, I used to walk five miles to school each day— uphill both ways!" Similarly, young and boastful New York

Mets fans have heard from their Brooklyn-born elders graphic descriptions of the manic celebrations that occurred when the Dodgers won their first World Series in 1955.

Reminiscence is not an objective, photographic image of past events. It is more a creative reconstruction of events that accommodates memories to meet a person's current emotional needs. Reconstructing one's past, for instance, can release a wealth of incidents with which a raconteur can embellish a narrative. A commentator once explained the fluidity of facts in one man's recollections in these terms: "They were all the same story, each told with the personality of the listener in mind."[3]

"Creative reconstruction" is an apt expression. It connotes that the process is likely to be spontaneous and only partially conscious. It is different from "deceitful," "lying," or "pathologically distorted" accounts. Reminiscences are the fruits of efforts to recover the past, with the understanding that the needs of the moment will affect the accuracy of what is recalled.

Reminiscence begins as soon as a child starts to remember things and continues throughout the life cycle. Studies, in fact, indicate that adolescents as a group spend the largest percentage of time in reminiscence.[4] This book, however, focuses on the reminiscences of older adults.

## Life Review

Life review has the same immediate, fluid nature that characterizes reminiscence. It is a form of reminiscence in which individuals reflect upon their personal history and accept responsibility for it. It is a process in which reviewers gradually reconstruct and assess their past, using their current values to weigh behavior that their memories progressively return to consciousness. It focuses attention upon the connectedness of their past with their current sense of themselves, evoking memories of formative experiences that influenced their personal development.[5]

Life review is seldom a coherent progression of memories. Usually it proceeds circuitously through reverie, reflection, dreams, diary or journal entries, correspondence, and story-telling. A critical evaluation of life experiences with the goal of integrating them in an acceptance of oneself here and now is the unifying theme throughout these recollections.

Older adults carry out their life review in their own way. Some may be highly aware that they are examining their past, others may feel vaguely compelled to mull over their past, and still others may almost inadvertently become caught up in life review. Some may engage in reflection as a private, introspective experience. In doing so, they re-experience the past without reactions from others that could modify their interpretation of events. Others may obsessively retell tales of times past. Most often, life review involves reviewers and listeners in a give-and-take exchange situated somewhere between these extremes.

Ian's experience illustrates the spontaneity of life review, its evaluative character, and private insights. Ian, sixty-six, is a vice-president of a pharmaceutical corporation. During lunch in the corporate dining room, he was regaling his colleagues with anecdotes about a vacation his family had taken a decade earlier to his ancestral home in County Cork, Ireland. It mattered to him that his colleagues not only respected him for his professional competence but also appreciated his wit and sociability. He concluded his account by reporting the reply of his ninety-five-year-old great-uncle to Ian's observation that members of the family lived to a great age in Ireland. "Sure," was the response, "around here we have to shoot a man to start a cemetery."

Ian's story started a round of anecdotes at the table, each intended to top the others. Indeed, the last tale before the end of lunch was the most amusing of all. Ian enjoyed it as much as the others and decided to yield the field for the day. Intermittently throughout the afternoon and on the train that evening, however, his thoughts returned to the esteem in which his family held the tellers of fine tales. He thought of the role models that had surrounded him on family holidays. He mused about the precedents that had guided him as a youth so compellingly upon the vulnerable course of honing his verbal skills as a competitive instrument. Gradually his reflections led him to recognize his error in viewing esteem and affection as a prize to be awarded, and only to the winner. He did not need to outstrip another to be appreciated for his humor. Another's ability did not diminish his. The snatches of life review that succeeded his original reminiscences guided him toward an awareness of the unquestioned assumptions that determined his stance toward others—that he had to win esteem and affection from others before he could attribute them to himself.

Ian's experience is typical of life review. Its insights followed from the day's events, drawing Ian to reflect upon the continuity of his past and present self. Then, depending upon his own style of responding to new ideas, he could have dismissed the intuition that something is amiss, or summoned memories of other conquests to confirm the value of his "winning ways," or, as he did on this occasion, tolerated the awareness that his own insecurities had been the driving force behind his sociability. Again, according to his style, he could have kept these ruminations to himself or shared them with others whose opinions matter to him. However subtly, the process can guide him gradually to the conclusion that he can love himself simply for being himself, without imposing any conditions at all.[6]

## Life Review among Older Adults

This section discusses the reasons why older adults, as a group, are drawn toward life review. Although adolescents have the highest incidence of reminiscence in general, life review in particular peaks during the fifth decade and continues its high incidence thereafter. Jung postulated that during middle age, people undergo a psychological shift from developing and asserting their personality to assessing the meaning and quality of their life.[7] At that time, life review becomes an essential process in achieving a psychic balance between these two orientations. More recently, Levinson has argued that a midlife awareness of personal mortality prompts individuals to reappraise their life, to determine how well they have met goals set earlier, and to plan for their future.[8]

Retirement is an event that ordinarily precipitates life review, and may also afford time for self-reflection. It often severs people from significant and gratifying roles and relationships. In doing so, it may endow memories of seemingly trivial events with value beyond their original character, since these memories remain as the principal links to a person's identity before retirement.[9]

The increasing proximity of death is a further incentive to life review. The relationship between life review activity and awareness of death can be seen even in younger persons, such as the fatally ill or the condemned, who are confronting death. Similarly, Ebersole observed among the very elderly an "urgency" to share their life review, which she interpreted as follows:

> In preparing to relinquish their own life they seem to feel compelled to carry out some anticipatory grief work. This would add credence to the belief that a life review is essentially part of letting go.[10]

Finally, life review assists older adults in performing three developmental tasks that accompany aging. Life review can be effective in enhancing their ability to (1) protect their sense of identity, (2) cope with the grief of personal losses, and (3) maintain their self-esteem.

## Continuity of Identity

Affirming the continuity of one's identity is a task with several dimensions. For the past, it requires the readiness of older adults to take responsibility for their life story, and to locate it within the historical and cultural context that conditioned its progression. For the present, it includes the ability of older adults to savor still the satisfactions that they derived throughout the life cycle, and to forgive themselves for the harm they did and the good they did not do. For the future, it includes the capacity of older adults to anticipate their needs and plan for the most satisfying ways to meet them.[11]

In the following example, notice how Ethel draws upon all three dimensions to understand—and affirm—an emotionally difficult decision she has made. Her husband and she were both sixty-eight years old and lived in the same house in which they had raised their four children. Nine years before, they had it renovated so their divorced daughter and her children could live there in a separate apartment. At the time of the renovation, Ethel's mother was living in her own apartment nearby. She told Ethel she was suffering from lung cancer and had about nine months to live. She subtly and repeatedly indicated that she preferred that Ethel should take her into her own home or else into the new apartment. Ethel skirted her mother's muted request. Four months later her mother died in her own home at a moment while Ethel was shopping.

Ethel gave a graphic description of her resistance to her mother's muted requests to move. She recalled her heart racing, her body feeling bound to her chair, her mind frozen. In retrospect, she sometimes felt she had betrayed her mother, sometimes that she accelerated her death, sometimes that she was a coward for not directly saying, "No." She was depressed that she had "played this game" with her mother.

She lightened enough to say that the intensity of her reaction to her mother should have been no surprise. She recalled her mother's lifelong dysfunctional model for resolving differences. She simply made unilateral decisions without any consultation. Ethel's father would come home to find a new couch in the living room or an immigrant cousin moved into the guest room. Her parents would shout at each other for two days and live silently for two weeks. In the end, the mother's decision held fast. When Ethel, as an adolescent, protested that her mother should talk important decisions over with her father first, her mother replied, "What? And have *two* fights!" Although Ethel might disagree with her mother, she had, nonetheless, made her mother's reluctance to talk over differences an integral part of her own style.

It was not surprising, then, that over the years, Ethel developed a pattern of relating to her mother that held little intimacy. Though she never failed to attend to her mother's material needs, she took no steps that would encourage a caring openness between them. Now, as her life review disclosed the overlays of modeled behavior and conflicted feelings that influenced her behavior with her mother, it also helped remove both mystery and guilt from Ethel's decision not to take her mother into her home. With the emphasis each woman placed on asserting autonomy, their behavior had consistently confirmed that in the end they would choose to maintain their distance, emotional and physical, rather than further strain the bond between them.

## Coping with Current Stresses

When older adults confront current problems, many regularly review their lives for instances of successful problem-solving conduct. These precedents support their self-concept as competent people and serve as a model of effective behavior that they can adapt to their current situations. It is not unusual, as pointed out, for older adults to reconstruct the content of their recollections to better meet their present needs.[12]

Monica is an example of an older person who adapts effective precedents from her past to enhance her current coping ability. She is a seventy-one-year-old widow, retired from a successful law career. Though she is proud of her self-sufficiency, a hearing impairment and severe arthritis indicated that she finally needed to contact the local senior citizen center to arrange for home care services that would enable her to remain in her own home. She had resisted this notion for two years because of its inconsistency with her self-image and the bother she foresaw in dealing with the personnel who would enter her life. During the two years, however, she began recalling a series of incidents with a common theme: in the past she had regularly protected her own independence by appropriately calling upon the services of others.

She remembered her first week as a newlywed in a third floor walk-up apartment. She had spent one entire day in housecleaning chores. Faithfully following the directions on every aerospray can, she threw none that had any propellant left in it into the incinerator. At the day's end, she discharged each can into the toilet bowl. Before she could finish, however, her husband returned home and excused himself to wash up in the bathroom. When he extinguished his cigarette in the bowl, the vapors exploded, projecting him head first into the sink and knocking him unconscious. Despite the panic that seized her, Monica ably used the directory assistance to obtain ambulance service and expedited the attendants' efforts in rushing her husband to the emergency room. The episode became part of the family folklore, with Monica both the butt of humor and an example of a person capable in an emergency. This recollection elicited others with the same lesson—that she was experienced in taking care of herself by reaching out for help when she needed it. Her increased dependency at this point in her life need not mean she would become any less resourceful on her own behalf.

The social dimensions of life review, sharing memories with confidants or in a group, also provide resources when an older adult's "cope runneth over." Fellowship allows older adults to glean advice without appearing vulnerable, to learn about alternative problem-solving strategies, to have their own referral service, or to find a colleague ready to chauffeur, repair, or perform some other favor they can return in kind. It is not surprising that older men who reminisce are found to be less depressed than those who do not. Some of the best adjusted older adults enjoy storytelling and the social relationships it promotes.[13]

Other studies have confirmed the positive impact of this social dimension upon the cognitive functioning of older adults living in the community and upon the reality-orientation of confused nursing home residents.[14] In one nursing home, weekly group sessions began with memories of childhood and progressed chronologically through adulthood. By the conclusion of the project, its sponsors reported that:

> Participants reviewed some of their heritage; they exercised their cognitive and memory functions; and they seemed to grow in self-esteem and in each others' eyes by virtue of talking and being listened to in the group. They socialized while recalling past accomplishments and pleasant times.[15]

These are compelling benefits for people who are bearing the ultimate assault upon their coping ability, attacks upon their capacity to stay in touch with themselves and their environment.

## Maintaining Self-Esteem

Life review helps older people who have been dissatisfied with their past to work through those conflicts and continue their personal development.[16] The model for growth is seldom a straight line. Development, rather, generally proceeds through a series of ascending spirals that "dip to rise." The "dips" consist of those transitions during which people experiment with assumptions, problem-solving strategies, and points of view that evoke considerable anxiety. The "rises" consist of higher levels of performance, interactional skills, and self-esteem that are achieved and maintained because people have borne the anxiety and found it an inaccurate measure of their ability.

Cornelia was pleased to explain how she had used life review "to dip to rise." She was a vigorous eighty-year-old woman who had never married. She portrayed herself through a sequence of reminiscences as "efficient, proper, and caring," a lifelong "churchy" person who even now lived in a housing project across the street from the parish church that was the center of her social activities.

The "dips" she experienced were church-related. In one case, she had attended a parish renewal program during which a speaker had encouraged parishioners to arrive early for the Sunday service and use the time "to pick a person, not a pew." The following Sunday she dutifully entered the back of the church five minutes earlier than usual. As she began to walk slowly up the aisle, scanning the pews for a person "to pick," she discovered no one whom she especially wanted to befriend. Pew after pew she passed by—squirming children in one, a creditor in another, an inappropriately attired adolescent, a gossip, an unattended bachelor. Suddenly she was at the front pew and there, asleep, was a disheveled stranger who had taken shelter from the weather an hour before. By default, she "picked" the stranger, who remained asleep as the service began. He slept even through the homily, and was awakened only when an usher nudged him with a basket at the beginning of the collection. Then, suddenly, when the usher was six pews further back, the stranger jumped up, faced the congregation, and addressed the usher, "Oh, waiter! Waiter!"

Laughter swept the congregation, but Cornelia didn't laugh. Her reluctance to "pick" anyone that morning had provoked a new awareness of the barriers that her predilections erected to reaching out to others. She rose beside the stranger and observed kindly that they were in a church. He flushed and looked for an exit. She escorted him to a side door and invited him home for brunch. It was the first time in fifty years that she missed a Sunday service but she knew that at that moment she was finally "picking a person." She smiled at an emerging pun to add, "And I've been working at being less 'picky' every since."

## Reducing the Risk of Depression from Life Review

Depression is the primary risk accompanying life review when older adults do not share their assessment of their personal history with people they trust. For everyone, to some extent,

> life review, by its very nature, evokes a sense of regret and sadness at the brevity of life, the missed opportunities, the mistakes, the wrongs done to others, the chosen paths that turned out badly. The therapist sees anxiety, guilt, despair, and depression. In extreme cases, persons may become terror-stricken, panicked, and even suicidal, particularly if they have irrevocably decided that life was a total waste.[17]

Confidants and professional caregivers, however, can provide a perspective and affirmation that forestall an escalation from "regret" to "despair." Chapter 3 explains in detail how exchanges with caring listeners enable reviewers to check the appropriateness of their conclusions.

The role of trusted listeners is all the more crucial when older adults engage in life review while they are enduring current traumatic losses, such as a disabling condition, unwanted change of residence or death of a spouse. Their current decrease in life satisfaction can elicit a preoccupation with exaggerated memories of defeat or failure in their past. The distortion in memories cannot be addressed so long as reviewers do not share them with others.

While listeners can diminish these risks for most older reviewers, geropsychiatrist Robert Butler notes that there are three groups of older adults whose life review should be closely monitored by mental health professionals. One group consists of those who "have consciously exercised the human capacity to injure others."[18] Many of these people cannot imagine that they could be forgiven by those whom they have injured or by God. They feel no recourse exists to undo the personal or societal harm they have inflicted, to provide restitution, or to draw a modicum of good from the evil they have perpetrated. Often they appear obsessed with a theme or event, discussing it with one listener after another.

Butler describes a second group for whom life review is likely to be hazardous. This group, which he identifies as "characterologically arrogant and prideful,"

> may overlap with the previous group, but not all its members necessarily have undertaken directly hurtful actions. Their narcissism is probably particularly disturbed by the realization of death.[19]

Members of this group use life review not to appreciate the gratifications their memories recall, but to accentuate that their accomplishments and sources of life satisfaction are now behind them. Moreover, because they have built their self-esteem upon recognition for their achievements and affiliations rather than on their inherent worth as human beings, they view aging as distancing them further from the bases for their self-worth.

A third group of older reviewers vulnerable to depression consists of those who have tended throughout their life to live for the future. Their memories surface a lifetime of opportunities missed because they were focusing upon tomorrow rather than upon today. Feeling powerless now to modify on their own their future-orientation, and seeing death as foreclosing further opportunities, they despair over a life that appears to them wasted.

Older adults in these three groups should be referred to mental health professionals.

## Conclusion

Reminiscence and life review are familiar and effective processes that older adults use to protect their identity, to cope with current stresses, and to promote their self-esteem. For a minority of older adults there are mental health risks involved in life review that arise from personality characteristics or from a lack of opportunity to share their memories with another. Gerontologically prepared mental health professionals can assist older adults in coping with these problems.

This chapter has focused primarily upon the functions of life review and the conditions that precipitate reminiscence. The family contexts of life review—the themes, events, and relationships that it summons to mind—are the subject of the next chapter.

# 2

# A Family Context for Life Review: You Do Go Home Again

## Introduction

Experiences of life review invariably evoke memories of family episodes and folklore. This chapter introduces the concept of "life plans" to explain how this "homing" orientation of life review assists older adults in assuming responsibility for the conduct of their lives, evaluating themselves and kin with greater empathy, and using their insights for the benefit of younger generations. The chapter also presents the concept of "life plans" as a master theme professional caregivers can draw upon to enhance the life review process. Finally, the chapter examines the variety of techniques by which families transmit these "life plans" over generations. Experiences of life review that reveal the lifelong influence of these transmission techniques often help older adults to understand the personal behavior they regret but continued to repeat despite themselves.

## Family Origins of Each Person's "Life Plan"

A life plan is a design for an individual's life that ensures that the person will act out some of those themes which, for better or worse, have characterized the lives of family members over generations. It is a kind of format by which a family perpetuates its identity by replicating family traits in members of subsequent generations.

To use an analogy, it is akin to a "script" for one of the parts in the long-running family drama. Through a variety of techniques we shall examine in the following section, families assign their members the role of a particular character. The integrity of the drama then weighs upon members to remain in character, faithful to their "lines." In actuality, life plans allow for more individuality than does a script. Members can elaborate upon their parts, enter and withdraw from the stage on their own initiative, and improvise their lines. To varying degrees, families provide latitude in these respects, so long as members remain true to their character. Family members with an alcoholic life plan, for instance, may eventually live sober lives, but they should expect that their reputation for disrupting the lives of their kin will follow them nonetheless.[1]

Life plans that promote dysfunctional behavior generally emerge as the product of two components of family life, "toxic issues" and the "triangles" they engender. Issues are labeled "toxic" when they recur in families over generations because they are never resolved. Instead of coping with them when they arise, family members react with a heightened anxiety, which spurs demonstrations of denial, projection, and somatic symptoms. These defenses, in turn, amplify the fear that efforts to address the issues will impose strains on family relationships that are certain to sunder the family. The disproportionate number of abusive parents and alcoholics who were raised in families with an abusive or alcoholic parent testifies to the intractible resurgence of toxic issues.

Family sensitivity can raise any issue to a level of toxicity. The most consistent toxic issues include *wealth* (How much is enough? Who has access to it? How is it to be used?), *health* (use or avoidance of preventive and rehabilitative services; hypochondria; phobias), *sexuality* (knowledgeability; homophobia;

premarital and extramarital activity; scrupulosity), *work* (work-aholism; avoidance of work; a process or product orientation toward work), *anger* (forms of expression; targets; passive aggressiveness), *religion* (freedom to participate or disaffiliate; openness to challenges to institutional tenets), and *autonomy* (What decisions are mine to make? Where can I live? How often am I expected to contact kin?)[2]

One authority refers to toxic issues as "islands of sensitivity" in a family. When family members even approach one of the "islands," no more than a particular kind of look, a gesture, a word, or a tone of voice is needed to arouse an emotional explosion.

> A calm discussion in a family can touch on one of these islands, and before you know it the family is on an emotional roller coaster. One issue leads to the next, nothing is discussed to conclusion; charges lead to countercharges and attack to defense, feelings mount and chaos ensues.[3]

Issues that arouse such heightened anxiety are acted out in subsequent generations, sometimes in consecutive generations. Older adults, for example, may be able to identify three or four consecutive generations of family households with an alcoholic member. Other times, however, overt behavior may occur in alternate generations. The adult child of an alcoholic parent may abstain from drinking and prohibit it in his or her home to express resentment over the pain that the parent's drinking inflicted and to demonstrate loyalty to the non–alcohol-abusing parent. Although the drinking does not occur in this generation, the toxicity of the issue ensures that it will reappear, likely in the next generation. This "dry" household is not indifferent to alcohol consumption, and drinking remains a value-burdened issue, a bomb that something as commonplace as adolescent rebellion may detonate among the nondrinker's children.

When two family members feel that a toxic issue threatens the relationship between them, they draw in a third party to stabilize the original dyad. This third party may be an individual (spouse, child, paramour), several people (in-laws, bowling team, supervisors), an object (beach house, racing car), or an issue (political affiliation, time away from the family) that a twosome uses to "avoid facing the real, threatening, scary issues between them."[4] The original parties can now displace their unhappiness upon the "safer" issues arising from the triangle.

In a triangle, one party is eventually perceived as a "persecutor," acting overtly in a manner that troubles the second party, an apparently innocent "victim." The third party intervenes between the other two as a "rescuer." In the end, however, the intervention neither helps the victim to take care of himself or herself nor modifies the persecutor's behavior. Instead, it further locks the three parties into their triangulated positions and diverts attention from the dyad's inability to work through the original toxic issue.[5]

Furthermore, triangles so focus the parties' attention upon the actions of each other that each tends to discount his or her contribution to the maintenance of the triangle. This myopia leads the members to blame one another, rather than to accept responsibility for maintaining their own dysfunctional roles. Family therapist Thomas Fogarty makes the point:

> All members of a triangle participate equally in perpetuating the triangle and no triangle can persist without the active cooperation of all its members. One of the first lessons a child learns in life is how to parlay a potential triangle.[6]

Collusion abets everyone's self-interest. A husband, for instance, who is reluctant to respond to his wife's needs can subtly foster an overinvolved relationship between his wife and daughter. The wife, in turn, can accept the compensatory gratification from this relationship rather than confront her feelings of abandonment when her husband withdraws. The daughter, too, finds benefits in this arrangement. She may have privileges inappropriate to her age or enjoy being an intimate companion to her mother.

Triangles may have different configurations depending upon the toxic issue that precipitates their formation. A father may "persecute" a daughter when the issue involves her social life, yet also be "the victim" of her refusal to accept a position in the family business. However, once family members have committed themselves to a position around a specific toxic issue in their family of origin, they tend to keep this same position whenever that issue arises in other emotionally charged relationships, such as with a spouse, children, in-laws, friends, or colleagues.

Bob found in his own life review an example of a recurring triangle. He identified himself as a rescuer who played a stabilizing function between his parents, who were estranged over any subject involving finances. His mother (victim) invested in a compensatory relationship with Bob, while his father (persecutor) maintained a deprecatory attitude toward him. Bob, in turn, rallied toward his mother. Later, with his own spouse and children, he remained sensitized to expressions of anger, even of disagreement. He was unable to resolve arguments and felt drawn to one family member against another, all the while believing he must work everything out among them. Not surprisingly, he held a second job to ensure that he could meet the financial requests of his wife and children.[7]

A dysfunctional life plan, then, proceeds from a family's inability to resolve its toxic issues. Those children who become enmeshed in triangles arising from these issues tend to repeat their troubling role whenever the specific issues recur thereafter. Older adults in their life review eventually confront the misfortunes that have ensued from their own life plan. Appreciating the processes through which their families transmitted life plans from one generation to the next helps older adults understand the influence their own life plan has had upon their behavior.

## Transmitting a Life Plan

Life review can reveal the processes that originally enmeshed individuals in their life plan. It can disclose the variety of family techniques used to identify to children the toxic issues in the family, to convey the heightened anxiety associated with the issues, and to involve them in family triangles related to the toxic issues. Families generally use combinations of techniques to assure that these lessons come across. The most common techniques are discussed here.

*Lecture.* Older adults can usually recall many instances of lectures they received as youths that were intended to convey verities to which the lecturers were deeply committed (toxic issues). There may have been a dramatic incident that precipitated a lecture delivered on a specific occasion. The emotional intensity with which it was given, the awkward pauses and nonverbal signals of discomfort that accompanied emotionally loaded topics like sexuality, or the formal stiffness of the presentation, all convey the earnestness that was compressed into the lecture.

Rosalynn, for example, remembered that during the day of her fourteenth birthday her mother sat next to her on the sofa. She cleared her throat, and with a flourish of peroration indicated that she wanted "to bring up a few matters" that she hoped Rosalynn would keep in mind whenever she might be fond of a particular young man. She advised her daughter to observe whether the young man or members of his family had webbing between the fingers or toes or under the armpits. Should she notice this phenomenon, she should discontinue the relationship. She went on about a friend who had "mothered a monster" from a relationship with such a man. When she finished, her mother sought no feedback and left to finalize arrangements for the birthday party.

This was the closest that Rosalynn's parents came to providing sex instruction. Sixty-six years later Rosalynn can recall that her own reaction at the time was consternation that sex must be so dangerous that her mother needed to shelter her from any further introduction to the subject.

Older adults should be encouraged to ask the following questions to facilitate their recall of lectures from their youth:

*How did my parents compliment me?*

*How did my parents criticize me?*

*What was their primary advice to me?*

The answers to these questions tend to elicit, in turn, memories of subsequent situations that confirm or challenge the accuracy of the parent's remarks.

*Role Model.* June's experience reveals the influence that role models can have in transmitting toxic issues. She retired prematurely from her medical career because of nervous exhaustion. When she explains her reasons for having chosen public health as her area of specialization, she invariably mentions her mother's example. Her recollections begin with their walks to and from her kindergarten classes when her mother repeatedly stooped to pick up rusting nails and shards of glass from the sidewalk "so they can't hurt anyone" (rescuer). Through varied examples of compulsive behavior, her mother conveyed the point that a helpful response to people's needs was never enough (toxic issue). *Anticipating* people's need and removing obstacles to self-fulfillment were the authentic indicators of genuine concern for others.

Older adults should be encouraged to elicit memories of role models who have influenced their own life course by paying attention to the ways in which younger family members are now imitating behavior and attitudes they have modeled. Finding themselves now in the equivalent position of those who had been their own role models, older adults can more readily empathize with those who preceded them.

*Emotionally Loaded Terms.* Monique is a retired Baltimore school teacher who lives in Miami Beach. She reported that she grew up without hearing the word "Jews" spoken in her home. Her relatives referred to Jews exclusively as "kikes" and "hebes." As a child she heard her father, who spoke ill of no one, call Jews "Eskimos." He stopped the practice when she asked him for an explanation, but this puzzling designation conveyed to her that Jews must somehow be "very different."

As an adult, she became a civil rights activist on behalf of racially desegregated education. Her efforts regularly involved her in ecumenical and intergroup functions with Jews, blacks, and other minorities (toxic issue). Her activism was in part a reaction, she thinks, to her family's prejudices. In her own words: "Heads and tails—I'm acting out the other side of the same family coin."

Older adults can be encouraged to recall inflammatory epithets by noting intergroup experiences in which they participated or which were reported in the media that evoked especially intense visceral reactions in themselves. When they can simply stay with these reactions and avoid intellectualizing them or judging their appropriateness, they are likely to find epithets surfacing within themselves to express what they are feeling. Then, by immersing themselves in the power of the words, they may gradually elicit images of persons who years before used these terms in their presence.

*Family Folklore.* Family folklore often memorializes the participation of family members in events of national and international dimensions. Movements and events such as emigration, military service, economic depression, union organizing, natural catastrophes, or protests for civil rights may prompt a chain of anecdotes about kin whose behavior brought honor or dishonor upon the family. The criterion for judging their behavior is usually the fidelity with which kin are considered to have maintained family values and rules as they participated in these larger scenes. Read "fidelity" to mean "rescuer or victim/martyr," and "values and rules" to mean "toxic issues."

Such interpretations make it more evident how an emotionally charged concept like "family honor" becomes associated with a person's behavior in these movements and events.

Swen, for example, remembered clearly tales told of his maternal grandfather, an emigrant from Sweden in 1896. His grandfather had taken a menial job to survive. In the evening he attended courses in English and social studies in preparation for citizenship and the entrance examination for the fire department. On his off-duty hours, he closeted himself in the attic preparing for the civil service examinations that brought him through the ranks to battalion chief. Swen's mother even kept her father's fire fighter's blue shirt after he had traded it for an officer's white shirt.

Swen's grandmother had a heart condition that prevented her from pursuing a career of her own. She invested her ambition, instead, in her husband's ascendancy, so that his advancement actually reflected her will and his work. "Grandpa's legendary industry lives on," Swen bemoans. "Throughout my adult life I have been a novelist, all the while holding down another full-time job as well. I have driven myself as hard as he ever did. I know I did it to outstrip his own success. But today, I have more pencils than fingernails!"

Older adults should be encouraged to use family gatherings to invigorate their memories of family lore. Events that assemble the extended family, such as weddings, birthdays, anniversaries, holidays, and funerals, are occasions likely to stir nostalgia and family folklore. They provide opportunities to hear anecdotes that confirm, or complement, or challenge one's own renditions of the same tales. Older adults should note the folklore that others expect or ask them to repeat because it probably includes examples of the family heroes, heroines, and villains who epitomized or flouted the values and rules that matter to family members the most.

*Names and Nicknames.* Connotations associated with names and nicknames can further strengthen identification with a life plan. Kin, for instance, may look for a child who is named after someone in the family to repeat or exceed the accomplishments of his or her namesake. It has been suggested that "when families fight about whose forebears or whose side of the family the child will be named after, they're also arguing about the role they need or want this child to play.[8]

Robert, who recently retired as a pastor, cited the parental expectations that accompanied his name. He was named after his mother, Roberta, who had died of complications during his birth. His father idealized his mother thereafter. He refused to remarry out of deference to his wife's "sacrifice," and arranged for a memorial service each year on her birthday, wedding anniversary, and death. This service overshadowed Robert's own birthday celebration. He feels certain these associations with his name attracted him all the more powerfully to his religious vocation and to the self-effacement that impeded the constructive development of his talents within his vocation.

Older adults should be encouraged to assess the impact of a name or nickname by reflecting upon the person(s) whose name(s) they bear and looking for similarities with these namesake(s). Nicknames may especially have connotations, complimentary of unflattering.

*Family Slogans.* Maryellen locks her car doors before pulling out of the driveway, observing, "Better to be safe than sorry." Joel is stripped to the waist and wears a visor to screen the sun as he scrapes paint chips off the floor of the porch. "You know how it is, 'Idle hands are the devil's workshop.' " Yolanda, stylishly attired as always, declines a second eclair with a muffled aside: "A second on the lips; forever on the hips."

These aphorisms alert children to their family's definition of the "good life" and to toxic issues. They convey parental attitudes about an unlimited array of topics: enjoying one's body; the importance of appearances or of being educated, wealthy, or religious; how caring and anger should be expressed; how much self-expression is acceptable; how leisure time and savings should be used.

Older adults can be encouraged to raise their awareness of slogans that have influenced them by asking friends and kin about the slogans they most often hear them use, and by paying attention to the slogans that their siblings and children tend to use.

*Epitaphs.* "She married outside the faith." "He wouldn't spend a nickel to see an earthquake." "Her son killed himself." "She had a drinking problem for ten years." In each case a family member uses a cryptic statement, without qualifiers or elaboration, to summarize another person's life in terms of toxic issues in the family. It is irrelevant whether the person is alive or dead. The epitaph conveys the value judgment and interpretation the speaker has made about another. The tenacity of epitaphs once they have been spoken and the selection of only one or two criteria for assessing the worth of another person can make the impact of epitaphs intimidating.

Older adults can be encouraged to increase their awareness of the impact of family epitaphs upon their own life plan by asking themselves:

*"What would others write for my epitaph if I died today?"*
*"If I were to write my own epitaph, what would I say?"*
*"Whose epitaph is similar to mine?"*
*"What value judgments are contained in these epitaphs?"*[9]

*Sibling Constellation.* This concept concerns the influence that gender and ordinal position among siblings have upon relationships among family members. The nature of these relationships, in turn, affects the direction of each child's life plan. Consider, for example, the dynamics of three constellations, focusing upon a firstborn child, a middle child, and a youngest child. With the firstborn children, parents tend to be more anxious and restrictive, requiring more mature behavior than with laterborns (toxic issue). As a consequence of this differential treatment, firstborns tend to be conservative, "much more likely to live the parent's values, often a pleaser; that's the way they found their place, by pleasing the parents or adults, more likely to be protective or nurturant, more dominating, more likely to be a leader."[10]

The middle sibling learns from the parents and the firstborn about the family niche the older sibling has filled. After the birth of a second child, the family readjusts its patterns of interaction, and the new sibling has to learn to adapt to the roles that are in place. As a consequence, a middle child often develops better negotiating skills, as well as strong-willed tenacity, characteristic of someone determined to "catch up." Because the middle sibling also wants to "keep ahead" of the youngest, he or she frequently may experience life as a wearying competition that consistently precludes satisfaction with the latest accomplishments (life plan).

On the other hand, those youngest siblings who are flooded with attention from both parents and other siblings may be denied the opportunity of learning how to do for themselves. Overprotected youngest may then see themselves as powerless (toxic issue) and opt to "work around other family members to achieve their goals."[11] The interpersonal skills they develop under these circumstances contribute to their later popularity in roles outside their family.

Similarities in the gender and ordinal positions of parents and children in their respective generations can powerfully affect the kinds of expectations and prohibitions that parents convey to each child. Parents, for example,

> can identify more easily with that child of the same sex among their children that has a similar position to their own, and can relate more easily to that child of the opposite sex that has a similar position to a sibling of the parents.[12]

So too, a parent's sibling position can pattern the quality of relationships among the children. A mother who is herself an oldest daughter and had an estranged relationship with her youngest sister often witnesses the same difficulties recurring between her oldest and youngest daughters.

Older adults can be encouraged to appreciate the influence of sibling constellations upon their life plan by noticing the judgments that they tend to make of others on the basis of gender and birth order, such as, "She has such a bossy older sister!" Older adults can attend, too, to the judgments that siblings and kin make about them with reference to their birth order.

## Owning One's Own Life

At first sight, it might seem that when life review is concerned with family-based life plans, older adults would conclude that they have not progressed in wisdom and character but simply recycled programmed behavior throughout their life time. For a minority, those confirmed in their arrogance, narcissism, or vindictiveness, this conclusion does often lead to depression. For most older adults, however, life review elicits a paradoxical conclusion with which they affirm their past and find hope for their future.

The paradox develops as follows. As older adults review family interactions that enmeshed them in toxic issues, they also focus increasingly upon the ways in which they came to "own" the life plan passed on to them. They discern in their life review all the nuances with which they personalized their life plan. One older woman, for instance, tailored the life plan that propelled her to challenge authority by becoming a lawyer who specialized in cases concerning aliens and other immigrants. "Besides the issue of justice for this vulnerable population, I'd relish doing it all again," she waxed, "just for the vigor of the fight."

Older adults find in their life review examples of the myriad ways in which they actively affirmed their life plan and collaborated in maintaining it. Their families may have passed a life plan on to them, but they nurtured it for all the secondary gains it offered them. For example, after decades of substance abuse, one survivor recognized the "high" he had felt as the "savior" of his parent's troubled marriage. Each time he over-dosed, his parents would put aside their chronic quarrels to share their concern over his recovery. Of all his siblings, he was the only one during those decades who received the at-tention due a "martyred hero."

Moreover, many older adults find in their life review evi-dence of key lessons that were well learned, needed skills that were tested and honed, and courage against overwhelming odds—all consequences of their efforts to cope with the lia-bilities of their life plans. Reviewers discover not only how they have helped to sustain and manipulate their life plans, but also how they have even transformed them into a quixotic asset.

This had been Sybil's experience. She was a seventy-nine-year-old widow who for the past four years had her own apart-ment in a congregate living residence. The facility had a daily program of social activities and a comfortable refectory where the residents ate supper together. Sybil's neighbors sought her out as a colleague in their activities and a diner at their re-spective tables.

Sybil described her popularity in terms of the life plan she had inherited. As the firstborn child and only daughter, she had attended closely to her parents' expectations about the kind of adult she should become. First, appearances mattered. She had often heard her father sum up the quality of one of her friends with the epitaph, "lovely peaches and cream complex-ion," or heard her mother lament to a mirror that her own chin was "off center."

No less important was the charge to avoid controversy. She could not remember her parents ever arguing seriously with one another. They presented one mind about deeply felt opin-ions and usually socialized with others who agreed with them. They sent Sybil to private schools that would expose her only to the values they held dear.

Years later, Sybil admitted, she felt constrained to seek out shallow commonalities among friends and acquaintances, and avoid debating issues with those whose opinions differed from her own. She would have preferred to exchange her popularity for freedom from the panic attacks that smothered her unvoiced criticisms of others' opinions. She regretted, too, that she had kept the parameters of her world so small.

Gradually, Sybil warmed to her parents as she recalled the folklore about generations past. Her maternal grandmother had been the older sister of seven brothers. She had had to assist her mother with all the domestic chores, including the laundering and ironing of her brothers' clothes. Once she married, however, she put household tasks in the background. She devoted her energies to furthering her husband's career through frequent social events. For one of these events she cut off her daughter's waist-length auburn corkscrew and wore it as a fall. With such stress on appearances and actions before an adult public, there was little wonder that Sybil's mother was concerned about the location of her chin.

Sybil's paternal grandfather had dropped out of school after the fifth grade. He endured adult education and dancing lessons to win the hand of "a woman above his station." It was not surprising that it mattered so much to her grandparents that her father was the first in his generation to graduate from college. Sybil could understand later that he was only acting out of his vision of paternal duty on all those occasions when he corrected her pronunciation at the dinner table.

Her reminiscences did not decrease her panic feelings at the prospect of acting assertively. They did, however, put her life plan in perspective. She began to focus on the positive qualities of her life plan. Only the week before, she had befriended a neighbor who had started chemotherapy. Sybil had offered to accompany her to buy a wig, because she wanted her to "look good." She also began, in a small way with which she would be comfortable, to extend her personal boundaries. She took the initiative in selecting different tables at which to sit for supper. She savored these accomplishments and laughed at their modest scale, referring to her "heroism" in attempting them. She ended with this analogy: "You know, if you think of life as a poker game, my family dealt me a so-so hand, at best. Looking back, I may not have won the "kitty" at the game, but I give myself lots of credit for being able to stay in the game this long!"

This attention to the family transmission of life plans can also temper the severity with which reviewers evaluate themselves and others. In their life review, they can see how they and their contemporaries behaved in the very fashion that they criticized in others. Nieces, nephews, children, and grandchildren can find them wanting by the same standards that the reviewers applied to their forebears. Thus, the critique that older adults make of their own lives can lead them to greater empathy for behavior common to others.

Finally, this family orientation can draw older adults beyond their reminiscences to a greater concern with the wellbeing of younger generations. Older adults have lessons they have learned from their life review. They can anticipate the replication of toxic issues and triangles, slogans, and epitaphs among their grandchildren, grandnieces, and grandnephews. With this insight, they can try gently to modify their own patterns of interacting with younger kin in order to minimize the intensity of these phenomena. Dispassionately, even humorously, they can also point to their own lives as an object lesson concerning the influence that life plans can have.

It is not unusual, for instance, for extended families to include four generations. On the one hand, the longevity of older adults provides new opportunities for them to share the insights from their life review in a way that kin in younger generations can use to enhance their own problem solving and relationship-building skills. On the other hand, the family adjustments that adult children make as primary caregivers for parents who become frail can provoke a maelstrom of toxic issues and triangulated behavior. Under these circumstances, older adults may find alternative ways of interacting that will minimize their own contribution to these upsets.

Consider the tensions that are created when a two-generation household expands to include a widowed grandmother. Often either the grandmother or the mother feels pressured to abdicate her authority. In these circumstances, both sides use the child to protect their own interests.

> Grandmother, for example, may undermine mother's disciplinary authority and thus teach the child to see his mother as incompetent. Mother, on the other hand, alternately invites grandmother's help, and resists or rejects it because she loses her autonomy when the grandmother takes over.[13]

The situation is no less complicated when grandparents are called upon for child care following a divorce. They may raise their grandchildren as though they were their own children, and feel displaced if their adult child chooses to remarry.

Eileen's experience in a three-generation household illustrates the fruitful use of life review. She was an eighty-three-year-old widow when her son and daughter-in-law asked her to move into their home. Her heart condition was worsening and they had room available since fourteen-year-old Philip was the only child living at home. Eileen was ambivalent about the move because she knew her son and Philip regularly quarreled. Her poor health and her warm relationship with her daughter-in-law finally induced her to accept.

About two weeks after Eileen moved in, an argument broke out during dinner. Philip had responded in a sassy tone of voice to his mother's request that he mow the lawn the following day after school. Philip's father pounded the table, shouting his outrage about his son's audacity. Philip rushed outdoors and the others finished eating in silence. After everyone but the father had left the table, Philip returned with a hunting knife. He pointed the knife at his own chest and approached his father, crying, "I can't take it any more." The man remained relatively calm and persuaded his son to hand over the knife.

After an hour's give and take, father and son were reconciled. The father told Philip to apologize to Eileen for the scene at dinner. When he came to her room, Eileen thanked Philip for his courtesy, and then located the upset within the patterns of their family. Philip listened attentively as she spoke about her own father:

> "I think his temper was a smoldering fuse. He seldom exploded because the rest of us were too afraid to find out what it would be like. A hardness would enter his voice and he would grip one hand with the other. When he had this demeanor, we asked no questions, dropped what we were about, and did whatever he wanted.
>
> "When I married your grandfather against my father's wishes, he refused to attend the wedding. When the rest of the family came, he really hardened his heart. Only my children were able to bring him and me together—five years after the wedding.
>
> "I was more like a volcano. Outside the family, people loved me for being humorous and doing favors. I enjoyed my family, too, but there I'd get bothered when the children didn't do things the way I wanted and when I wanted them done. I knew about my temper, so I'd warn them by whistling for a while. If they didn't shape up then, I'd give it to them. I remember kicking your father twice. When he was twelve I gave it to him in front of the house because he hadn't practiced the cello that day. Then, when he was your age, I kicked over the kitchen chair he was on. He had been fooling around so much that he missed the bus for school.
>
> "Your father hardly ever acted up when he was a teenager. It worried me a little because I knew that he had to be burying his anger inside. Sometimes it would slip out. At his sister's graduation from college, he wanted my attention while I was talking to a friend. When I didn't stop right away, he dug his fingernails into my wrist. Another time, when he was sixteen, he pulled a practical joke that upset me terribly. His father and I came home from a movie to find him stretched out on the kitchen floor with a wound in his head. As soon

as I gasped, he jumped up and shouted, "Fooled you!" His wound was only catsup. He apologized after we told him how upsetting his ruse had been. He said he had gotten the idea from a comic book he was reading.

"I think he's better off now, fussing as he does with you instead of keeping it in. It's no picnic for you, I know, but you're doing better than he did at your age. I think you have the savvy to handle your father. After all, you knew it would get to him more if you pointed the knife at yourself instead of at him."

That was a graced moment for Philip and for Eileen. She used her life review to explain anger as a master theme in both their lives, to describe its permutations through the generations, and to raise the boy's empathy for his father. She used her own experience to illustrate the inevitability of excess and mistakes in coping with anger. Not least for Eileen, she avoided the snare of interjecting herself between father and son.

## Conclusion

Life review enables older adults to recall the processes by which their families transmitted a life plan for them to follow. Each family has an array of preferred plans that are passed on to preserve the family's identity and stability. Awareness of the family's intractible power throughout the life cycle of its members, however, can have a liberating effect. It can empower older adults to assume responsibility for their lives, to judge themselves and others empathetically, and to use the lessons from their life review for the wellbeing of the younger generation.

Such reflection upon the dynamics of relationships among family members, however, does arouse a welter of emotions, both gratifying and disturbing. Because this emotional intensity can interfere with the recall of memories and skew one's understanding of them, the presence of a confidant who can listen empathetically and accompany an older adult through life review is a precious resource. The following chapter is devoted to the skills and techniques that a confidant can call upon to provide such assistance for an older reviewer.

# 3

# Confidants: The Caring Listeners

## Introduction

Most older adults have one or more friends or family members with whom they can comfortably share their life review. These confidants are valued parties who ideally are short on advice and long on empathy, interested more in understanding than in judging. They are the listeners who make it easier for older adults to draw meaning and peace from their life review by the acceptance and support they provide.[1] This chapter examines the attitudes and skills that characterize such caring listeners.

The chapter discusses, first, the value of enlightened self-interest as a primary motive for a confidant's involvement in facilitating another's life review. It then explains techniques that confidants can use to stimulate a reviewer's recall of events, and techniques to help a reviewer who is "stuck" at some incident in the past, continually recounting it to weary ears. The chapter concludes with recommendations for helping older adults who are engaged in life review without benefit of a confidant.

## Incentives To Listen

Engaging friends or family members of older adults to listen attentively to the latter's life review is one of the most meaningful ways in which professional caregivers can enhance the life review process. In doing so, however, professionals need to emphasize that these confidants should listen to another's life review primarily *to benefit themselves*. This personal incentive generally has more staying power than altruistic motives when confidants eventually grow impatient with thrice-told tales, annoyed with a reviewer's seeming ingratitude, or distracted by reasons for extricating themselves from their role as audience.[2]

There are so many occasions when listeners will need to draw upon enlightened self-interest to cope with their own heightened anxiety. Older adults' life review may raise issues that are no less toxic for the listener than for themselves. Sometimes the listener may have strongly identified in a given issue with certain relatives from whom the reviewer is estranged. Other times a confidant may realize that he or she is currently distressed with an older reviewer over the same issue that the reviewer has identified as one especially painful to address.

These experiences are indicators to confidants of their sensitivity to turbulent issues that they need to address in their own lives. Happily, attention to their own sensitivity enhances their attentiveness to the life review being shared with them. When their primary objective as a confidant is reducing the control of a life plan over their own lives, confidants find it easier to listen without judgment to the life plan that appears in the review being shared with them. In fact, awareness of parallels between the reviewer's situation and their own tempers the readiness of listeners to offer glib advice or patronizing insights.

The experiences that Phyllis and Nellie had as confidants are examples of the value of enlightened self-interest as a motive for assuming a confidant's role. Phyllis, the middle of three sisters, looked forward to seeing the old family movies each Christmas when she returned to her Ohio home from Los Angeles. During her most recent visit, she again viewed the films together with other family members. After the others had retired, her mother shared with Phyllis reactions to the movies that she had always kept to herself. She mentioned the despondency she felt when she watched the oldest daughter, six years old in the film, "having a fit in front of everyone" because she was compelled to wear a hat to church on Easter morning. The despondency reflected the mother's interminable arguments with this daughter, even to the present. She recalled the satisfaction she felt when she filmed the tantrum as evidence of the "impossible behavior" she had endured from this child. Now, however, she regarded the filming of that scene as an act of "spitefulness" on her part rather than evidence of "long-suffering," and wished she could "mend fences" with her daughter. As Phyllis listened, she realized she had left home for Los Angeles because she had intuited that had she stayed, she would have been targeted to replace her sister in this harried relationship with her mother.

Nellie was a middle-aged woman who had internalized her father's rigid ethic that all duties for the day must be discharged before "rewarding" oneself with "idle" moments of relaxation. She now listened to his recollections for more profound insights into the rigidity of her own sense of obligation. One evening he shared his memories of a counseling session he attended when his children were adolescents. The counselor had asked him to give a symbolic representation of his own adolescent years. Here is the gist of his reply:

> His father was a Mississippi paddle boat proceeding upriver under full steam. His mother was a howling winter gale buffeting the ship. He himself was a buoy whose flashing light was needed to keep the paddle boat from running aground. He wanted to "be there" to prevent disaster, to be accessible "on site" for every hazardous condition. He felt so inadequate, however, being tethered, passive, a beacon who might be unseen or ignored.
>
> He translated these images into a vivid, real life scene in which his parents were quarreling violently over a toxic issue. His mother accused his father of stubbornly preferring am-

bition to family. His father responded in kind, dismissing his wife was "carping" and "disloyal." Nellie's father felt ignored throughout, anchored in oblivion. Though he was in the very next room, he did not know what to do. He so strongly needed to rescue them from their anger, but did not know what to say. Finally, before he could accomplish anything, his mother fled to her room.

Nellie learned more from that moment of shared review than she had ever imagined. She was not only her father's daughter, but her grandfather's granddaughter. There was less mystery now about the makings of her character. To know her family through her father's life review was to meet herself as well.

Enlightened self-interest is no less needed among participants in groups devoted to life review. Certainly the announced purpose of such groups facilitates self-disclosure, and similarities among reminiscences prompt further candid recollections from participants. Members are usually attentive, expecting to receive the same respect in turn. On the other hand, members may be poorly motivated for sharing memories at all, unless the group has been self-designed. The recollections shared may be those considered "safe," instead of being spontaneous and candid. Moreover, when personality conflicts occur among group members, the stories told may be presented more in competition with one another than for the insight they convey. Confronted with these distractions, members are more likely to contribute to the group's effectiveness when they perceive each other's reminiscences as resources that they can use on their own behalf.

## Facilitating Recall and Sharing of Memories

This section surveys techniques with which confidants can facilitate older adults' recall of memories. Sometimes the help that confidants provide may be as basic as "granting permission" to reminisce to those older adults who have been taught "that living in the past is a sign of senility."[3]

One man in his eighties, for instance, who resisted all suggestions as an invasion of his independence, would dyspeptically search his rooms for his eyeglasses rather than complain aloud that he did not remember where he had left them. He had labeled such complaints as overt symptoms of mental decline. Similarly, he refused to discuss his memories of any events that had occurred before Truman's presidency, since he regarded "rehashing old times" as the second most demeaning symptom. He eventually allowed himself to speak of the distant past only after his confidant, in his mid-forties, called to cancel their luncheon because he had inadvertently scheduled a dentist's appointment for the same time. The confidant's memory lapse defused the negative associations the older man had linked with "old folks' " behavior.

There are also tasks that confidants can carry out together with an older adult that prompt memory recall. They can accompany an older person on visits to the original homestead; solicit information about artifacts, souvenirs, heirlooms, and public documents like wills, mortgages, birth certificates that are in the person's possession; rummage together through picture albums; concentrate upon one specific theme at a time, such as the family's summer excursions or ways of celebrating holidays.

A visit to the original homestead tends to evoke a wealth of reminiscences. Seldom does the current scene match memories of how things used to be. Houses seem closer to the curb, lawns smaller, and vacant lots gone all together. These disparities engage older adults in sorting through memories, reflecting on the meaning that they hold for them now, and discerning the threads of continuity that join them to their past. When it is not possible to make such a visit personally, older adults can facilitate their recall by drawing the ground plan of their home with as much detail as they can. By locating windows accurately, they may recall the views that these windows faced and their own activities that could be seen from that viewpoint. By locating the furniture precisely, they may remember whose favorite chair that was and the quality of their interaction with that person.

The same flowing association of memories can result from a leisurely stroll through the neighborhood, past the primary and secondary schools, the parish church, and the teenage hangout. Older adults may want to make this visit to each house in which they have lived.

Many older adults have kept public documents that record crucial moments of their family history. There, in a bank's safe deposit box or in a file cabinet in the basement, are citizenship papers, birth and death certificates, marriage certificates, census ledgers, and titles of home ownership. Each has its own significance for the possessor and often different meaning for other family members. Older reviewers may feel moved to contact relatives for their perspectives about these documents.

Family artifacts, heirlooms, and souvenirs are even more evocative. They are regularly on display and are likely to have accompanied their owners wherever they have lived. A coverless Bible may be the only item preserved from ancestors' immigration. The reminiscences it elicits about the values and persons who kept it intact can also stir the older adult to decide who should receive it next.

The very familiarity of these pieces should challenge their owners to remember their significance. Consider the tarnished medal won in high school sixty-two years before. The recipient was one of four runners in the two-mile relay. The names and faces of the other three are available in the yearbook on the shelf. A vivid reverie begins, presenting races re-run, the hilarity and fellowship of training camps revived, and a heightened awareness of the place of competition in the reviewer's life.

Perhaps nothing prompts recall like photographs, music, and aromas. Pictures of the cars older adults have owned may measure their affluence and/or the demands of family size. Indeed, a picture of an open rumble seat in an ancient Pontiac may still provoke shivers at the memory of freezing journeys.

Pictures of cabinmates at summer camp precede those of vacations taken by the extended family in caravan fashion to a variety of national parks. Again a reverie begins, tracing the summer vacations through the decades and stirring interest to find snapshots for them all. Organizing reminiscences by themes such as the celebration of holidays, vacations, residences, employment, friendships, weddings, or any number of topics turns photo albums and old address books into resources.

Music has a similar effect. Patriotic tunes can arouse recollections of parades, marching bands at athletic events, and participation in political causes. Popular tunes from earlier decades can recall the vagaries of a youthful social life and more serious world events referred to in the lyrics.

As for aromas, there are older adults who can recall each kitchen in which they first sniffed a pie other than the kind that their mother baked at home. Even today they will speak of their oldest friends in terms of the cherry, blueberry, and pecan households that they came from.

Confidants who are also family members may prefer a recall strategem that pastoral counselor William Clements recommends.[4] He suggests that a confidant arrange a family gathering for the purpose of having members elaborate upon scenes significant in the history of the family.

> Only those events which are directly remembered could be used. Each participant would decide which personal memory is worthy and share it with the family group, who could then ask questions or add details from their own memories. The generations could be talking and listening to each other with a renewed appreciation for a shared history. Painful events as well as funny stories might all be part of the total experience.

In her book on preparing memoirs, Katie Wiebe offers a format for revivifying memories.[5] She encourages confidants to develop a time line with an older adult that integrates per-

sonal events from the reviewer's life with historical events. She
envisages a confidant saying the following to the reviewer:

> At one end put down the date of your birth and at the other
> end the present date. Now, at the appropriate points, locate
> the "firsts" and the main events of your life, such as the first
> Christmas you can remember, first illness, first school day,
> first love, first kiss, first job, first failure, first time you
> openly took a stand for some position, your marriage, births
> of children, deaths in the family that affected you, first spir-
> itual awakening, first public speech, first long travel, and so
> forth. On the other side of the line add events which were
> taking place in the world beyond your own, but which af-
> fected yours . . . As you do this, you will find still other
> memories coming to you to connect with these changes in
> the world beyond yours.

Confidants, of course, can also elicit reminiscences simply
by encouraging older adults to talk about the involvement of
family members in larger issues of historical or cultural significance. These commonly include immigration, natural dis-
asters, military service, economic depression, racial
discrimination, and long-distance relocations. Using these
themes, older adults can proceed from the larger topic to the
more specific details of events that involved their family. This
specificity, in turn, evokes sentiments and value judgments that
are at the heart of life review.

Tim provides an example of how this progression may occur.
This reticent bachelor was a seventy-four-year-old retired
plumber. He lived in a neighborhood so thoroughly Irish that
the city council had allowed the traffic signal at the main in-
tersection of the neighborhood to have the green above, and
the red below, the orange light. In response to questions about
Ireland's potato famine in the 1840s, he mentioned that his
maternal grandfather and siblings had immigrated to the United
States at that time in order to survive. He recalled the family
lore about the "American wake" his great-grandparents held

for their immigrating children that lasted through the night before they left. Each child danced and sang for the parents, and friends and neighbors visited to bid farewell. Tim's account mirrored a historian's summary, "After emigrants left their parents at the doorway, younger family members and friends accompanied them to the railroad station or a particular cross-roads. It was a funeral procession leading away from home."[6] Tim's story also contained an account of the passage over, with particular detail to the inadequate rations of water and the meager inches separating sleeping berths.

During two subsequent discussions, Tim elaborated upon the meaning this exodus held for him (an interpretation that has professional adherents as well). He felt that something in the culture encouraged a wariness toward intimacy. He recognized the wariness during his visits to Ireland when he saw the priority that young and middle-aged adults gave to same-sex friendship groups over intimacy with their own spouse. The pattern continued in the diaspora of those who emigrated, epitomized in the slogan his mother would recite when he complained of some abuse at the hands of fellow children, "Be pleasant to all, keep few friends, and trust no one."

Near Tim lived another unmarried septuagenarian. Kevin was initially no more expansive than Tim, until he started reminiscing about the reception that his Irish ancestors received in latter nineteenth century America. He recounted how his grandfather had been bludgeoned to death by private detectives during the "Long Strike" of 1875 in the Pennsylvania coal mines. He recalled his parents' stories about demeaning stage shows portraying stereotyped Irish characters who were profligate, childish, crooked, or drunk. His parents had reacted with a tenacious ambition for themselves and their children. Kevin himself had been a successful lawyer. As he expanded upon the consequences of this family theme, he grew more introspective. He spoke of each sibling, and described how the youngest brother had rebelled, only to adopt the caricature of the drunken Irishman. Kevin then ruminated about the consequences that continue to befall his family because of their intense reactions to anti-Irish stereotypes.

## Helping Reviewers Past Points of Repetition

It happens that a particular reminiscence may evoke an emotional response that then suffuses subsequent memories. An older adult may appear mired in this mood as though it had pervaded all of his or her life experience. Very likely this perseveration indicates that the person has not yet integrated the initial reminiscence as part of his or her personal history. In these cases, confidants are in a position "to prevent the reviewer from becoming stuck at some painful point in the past, . . . to disarm a guilty or hurtful recollection by reducing it to one small incident in the larger perspective of a lifetime."[7]

Confidants can help by attending non-judgmentally to the content that is shared with them. By accepting the interpretation that older adults attribute to the events remembered, listeners can respond to the need of reviewers "to be listened to on their own wavelength; otherwise they say they are not heard. A friend listens by taking seriously what they bring up again and again; he or she says, 'This is really important to you because you keep repeating it.' "[8]

Confidants can also help reviewers distinguish between the opinions and sentiments they had at the time an event occurred and those they hold now. Confidants can then affirm the reviewers' ability to proceed beyond a troubling event and yet return to it in reminiscence despite the discomfort involved.

Confidants can point out the impact of life plans and toxic issues upon older adults' behavior. On previous occasions, older adults may have judged their own behavior pejoratively, for example, as little more than timorous advocacy for someone oppressed, or disgruntled forebearance with someone inept, or slender hospitality to an unexpected guest. When these same incidents, however, are viewed against the family context that promoted their own life plan, they may now reassess their behavior. Now that they are aware of the constraints of their life plan, they may judge the same behavior as virtually heroic, as showing them acting at the limits of their capacity.

Roland is a case in point. Retired from a career as a successful business executive, he only recently concurred with his ex-wife's contention that through the three decades of their marriage he had valued competing with other men for corporate rewards more highly than attending to his relationship with her and their children. After discussing this pattern with his closest friends for some months, he began to share other "unpleasant" memories that had begun to gnaw at him. He remembered how time and again his mother had contrasted his achievements during high school and college with his father's modestly compensated career. Slowly his life review led to the insight that his priorities had, in fact, resulted from the life plan he had been following. He gradually came to accept what could not be undone, and finally began to temper the competitiveness to which he was still so powerfully drawn in his relationships with his own children.

Confidants familiar with the interactional patterns and heritage of an older adult's family of origin are in a position to be particularly helpful. They can recommend that kin who are knowledgeable about the events join in their discussion. Often these expanded meetings reach a consensus about facts that alter judgments based upon less reliable recollections. Sometimes the additional parties were even protagonists in the events and can distinguish between their sentiments at the time and how they feel about the events now.[9]

## Enhancing Life Review without a Confidant

There are many older adults without a confidant with whom they can share their life review. This absence has its disadvantages because it deprives them of the prompting, questioning, and feedback that confidants provide. With a modicum of self-discipline, however, these older adults can successfully use

most of the techniques included in this chapter to elicit reminiscences and review them from an intergenerational, family
perspective.

Tape recording a life history or personal journal is an effective technique to facilitate life review. Listening to these re-
cordings enables older adults to use the nuances of their own
inflections, tone of voice, vocabulary, and choice of content as
clues to reveal the assumptions, toxic issues, and life plans
nested in their life review.

A personal history or journal ideally includes a broad sweep
of topics and the memories associated with them. An elderly
shut-in who was recording the role of food in his life found
himself speaking about "the symbolism of food, food for the
holy-days, the ethics of food, food and power, food and love,
food and sex, comfort food."[10] Similarly, an older woman who
focused upon gender-based concerns in her personal history
covered such topics as menstruation, attitudes about sex, child-
birth, housework, relationships among women, reading materials intended for women, menopause, and women's
participation in public life.

The personal journal, as Ira Progoff has conceived it, has
been especially valuable in stimulating and deepening the life
review process. A proponent of the Progoff method describes
the affinity between this form of journal and the goals of life
review as follows:

> Too often we see our past as a bundle of excuses to explain
> or justify who we are right now. It becomes the foundation
> of our resentments, tastes, enmities, the excuse for our pres-
> ent behavior, good or bad . . . To heal memories with the
> aid of the journal, the trick is not to analyze the past but to
> help ourselves to reexperience it . . . When in memory and
> writing we face the situation once again, and fully feel its
> emotions, we can allow them and our response to them to
> fully run their course in the safe laboratory of our journal.
> There we can talk back to the situation and the people in it
> without hurting ourselves or others. This requires writing

in depth and detail, feelingful as well as factual. Often dialogues and letters are preferred strategies for the final working out of these past scenes that come to us in the course of daily journal entries.[11]

Journal writing is more a meditative than cognitive experience. An older adult begins by sitting quietly, trying to re-experience a past event that holds some special meaning. The journal then evolves as a "dialogue script" with another person who also participated in that event. Progoff describes the process:

> As we write, our inner attention is directed to the other person. We feel their presence, and thus they speak to us . . . We speak and we listen. The other speaks, and we record it as it comes to us. A *dialogue script* is forming itself.
>
> After we have written our dialogue script we return to stillness. We let ourselves become aware of the emotions we felt while the dialogue was being written. Whatever these were, we record them now as an addition to the dialogue. We make no judgment and no interpretation of them . . . We may now wish to take the further step of reading it aloud, and especially of hearing ourselves read it.[12]

Reading the journal entry aloud usually evokes powerful emotions the reviewer should not restrain. These feelings are noted in the journal and become, in turn, a source that will conjure up still further reminiscences.

Mitzi's use of a journal illustrates its benefits. She was a seventy-eight-year-old single woman who resided in a nursing home for the last seven years of her life. Because a degenerative condition prevented her from writing and required her to receive institutionalized care, she tape recorded the entries for her journal. Because she was an only child, she had arranged that upon her death the journal should be mailed to a cousin reputed to be the chronicler of the extended family's history.

She chose her high school graduation as an event that epitomized her adolescent years. During that ceremony she was awarded a scholarship to a university in Connecticut. She remembered the exhilaration of knowing the award would relieve her parents of a heavy financial burden and allow her to buy a car of her own to commute the seventeen miles to the campus. She recalled her anticipation about attending a school of veterinary medicine after she completed her major in biology. She remembered, too, how insignificant the demands of her Saturday job at her father's grocery seemed at that moment in comparison with this liberating news. Though her father had died twenty-three years before, she knew she had to talk with him in her journal about the memories associated with her high school graduation.

Mitzi said she was drawn to her father at that moment in the hope that this would be the time when she could decipher the welter of emotions that had disturbed their relationship. She told him now she hated working at his grocery on Saturdays, packing the orders that she would later deliver to customers' homes. Either she stayed home on Friday nights or staggered through Saturday on three hours' sleep.

She thanked him for never even asking her to help, for letting her sleep that extra hour after he had left for the store, and for his admonition between customers (even if it turned out not to be true), "The more schooling you get, the easier time you'll have making a living." Then, her voice choked as she explained that she had felt no choice but to help after he had suffered his heart attack. She had set her mind to help after she had found him on the bus asleep one night when she returned late from a school activity. He took up so little space huddled in his seat and would have gotten home who knows when had she not awakened him.

Her voice softened as she spoke her father's reply. He thanked her and added that he noticed how she did the work of two adults. He asked if she recalled how proud he was to introduce her to his customers. He ended by saying that he did not begrudge his own years of strenuous work because he knew that he had lost his options when he dropped out of high school.

The spontaneity and intensity of her rage startled her. She stammered into the recorder that it was his own fault to have quit school. That decision had painfully affected the entire family. His schedule had robbed them of his company. She had often heard her mother confront him, crying, "Just for once, put me first!" Then, following his heart attack, Mitzi, too, became caught in his grocery trap.

Her father answered, still softly. He reminded her of another episode when she had accompanied him to visit his father during his final illness. Toward the end of the visit, she had left the two men alone. When her father later left the bedroom, she had observed his sullen anger over some exchange that occurred between the men. That's how it had always been— a cutting word from the father and a smoldering retreat by the son. Early on he had resolved never to ask his father for any kind of help. When his own resources were not enough, he would double the hours he put into his work.

The recorder caught Mitzi's sigh of recognition. Her grandfather's stringent style helped her understand her father's insistence upon being self-employed, even at jobs that seemed to consume them all.

Mitzi told her father that she imitated him too well. After his death, she had taken employment in town that supplemented her mother's income. She abandoned her plans for veterinary school, lived at home, and eventually became her mother's primary caregiver. She recognized that her responsibility for this series of decisions was the issue sticking in her throat. It was an issue made more complicated, she could see, by the way she had identified with her mother's feeling of being "second fiddle" to her father's workaholism. She had originally seen duty and work as a family curse. But now she no longer needed to blame her father, or anyone, for that matter. She would take credit for her own decisions and their consequences.

Mitzi's journal continues for eleven more tapes. They reveal how she approached the peace that can follow upon a patient attentiveness to accounts of past events and to the voices in the dialogues. She had made the journal a worthy confidant.

## Conclusion

Ideally, life review is a shared experience in which older adults can benefit from the questions and opinions of friends or family members. Such confidants need an array of skills to facilitate the reviewer's recall of distant or disturbing events, and to assist in putting these memories to the service of forgiveness and self-esteem. By drawing upon self-discipline when confidants are unavailable, older adults can use these skills themselves to enrich their life review. The Progoff model of journal writing is especially effective when older adults are carrying out life review in isolation.

Discussion of skills and techniques introduces the next chapter, which is devoted to the use of poetry as an aid to life review. Poetry is an accessible and accommodating resource enhancing life review that older adults can use privately, with a confidant, and in groups in which participants discuss their selections of poetry and the themes that these selections evoke from their past.

# 4

# Poetry: A Gentle Tool for Life Review

## Introduction

Many older adults find that poetry is an inexhaustible resource that revives significant memories, captures the emotional tone of scenes from their past, and expresses the meaning that these scenes now hold for them. This chapter first examines rhyme as a mnemonic that associates a poet's themes and images with relationships and events from the lives of older adults. The chapter then explains how poetic themes and images about the wisdom among older adults, about reminiscing, frailty, family relationships, providence, and death can assist older adults in finding meaning and comfort in life's most telling moments.

Poetry is a bountiful source of engaging images. Some older adults have already identified favorite verses that express a dominant theme in their lives. The verses may be chosen from the works of their favorite bard or selected from poems treating a treasured subject, such as nature's beauty, marital and parental ties, or perseverance in adversity. Others, who may earlier have been indifferent to poetry, are often attracted later to images that recapture a deeply felt experience from their own lives. Many begin to express the insights and emotions arising from life review in poetry that they compose themselves.[1]

Human service professionals appreciate the flexibility that

poetry offers in their work with older adults. Older clients can refer to poems on their own initiative as well as part of a group function. Groups are readily organized in both institutional and community settings. Few materials are needed beyond anthologies or mimeographed selections.

## Rhyme

Rhyme itself sometimes explains attraction to an image. It anchors an image in memory, facilitating the reviewer's recall of an event or theme and attracting other associated events that converge upon the image.

Sean, an older member of his Elks Lodge, provides an example of the convergent power of rhyme. He was a member of a life review workshop sponsored by the lodge. When the topic of using poetry arose, Sean observed that the only poetry he could recall consisted of brief excerpts that he remembered because they were "held together at the ends of lines." He then recited from *An Essay on Man: Epistle III* by Alexander Pope:

> *Man, like the gen'rous vine, supported lives;*
> *The strength he gains is from th' embrace he gives.*

He savored the memories of his mother and his youth that the theme of this verse evoked for him. After his recent retirement as an executive in California's silicon valley, he decided to make a Christmas visit to his grandchildren who live in Manhattan. To use the several hours of idle time between the arrival of his flight and the time when one of his grandchildren would be home from work, he drove to the neighborhood where he had lived as a child. He passed the elevated subway line and his grammar school, and arrived at his childhood home. When he rang the doorbell to request permission to walk up the driveway to take photographs, a woman in her fifties answered the door. After he had identified himself and explained his purpose, she mentioned the complimentary manner in which her neighbors had always spoken of his parents. She introduced herself as Naomi Stein and invited him in to see the house.

On one wall in the living room hung a very large painting of an elderly man with a flowing beard. When Sean commented on the striking portrait of the old man, Mrs. Stein said it was of her grandfather, copied from an old photograph.

As she pointed toward the picture, the tattooed number from a concentration camp was evident on her arm. Sean stammered his regret about her internment. She responded that her grandfather and sixty-seven other family members had died there. She welled up as she told of other misfortunes that had beset her family during the decade they had lived at that address. Then she caught herself, and remarked that surely Sean had tales of happy family times in the house that he could share with her. From a reservoir of fond recollections, he recounted anecdotes pertinent to each room through which they passed.

At the top of the stairs, however, on the landing outside the door to his childhood bedroom, he fell silent, recalling his father's death. This was where he had met his mother when she came tearing out of her bedroom, shrieking that his father had died and banging her hands against the wall. While he was flooded anew with the pain, Mrs. Stein said, "I'm so glad you came here today. By sharing your happy memories, I feel connected to this house at last. I can be happy here now, too." "That's terrific," he replied, keeping his own feelings at that moment private. He reviewed the other rooms and then departed. Mrs. Stein's reaction had irrevocably introduced a new, and consoling, dimension into the memory of his father's death.

The lesson for Sean was not simply that current reality may not conform to recollection. Rather, he learned how the past is subsumed and interpreted within the context of present experience. The remembered grief of his mother and himself is now fused with the relief that his visit brought to Mrs. Stein.

For Sean, Pope's lines evoke the comfort of this resolution each time he repeats the rhyme.

## Wisdom

Many poems exalt the wisdom of older adults. The following participants in a foster grandparent program found several examples that they adapted to their own lives. They met weekly at nearby grammar schools with the children they befriended. A consultant to the program included in her group interviews with the foster grandparents an inquiry about poems that had special meaning for them.

Raoul, seventy-nine, had seven grandchildren of his own and two fifth graders in the program whom he had "adopted" three years before. He brought an excerpt from Alexander Pope's *An Essay on Man: Epistle IV* which he read:

> *Tell what is it to be wise?*
> *'T is but to know how little can be known;*
> *To see all others' faults, feel our own.*

Raoul had often felt that the guardians of his foster grandchildren erred in their handling of problematic situations with the youngsters. He said this verse had alerted him to avoid with these children the mistakes he had made in compounding troubled relationships that existed between his own children and grandchildren. He had learned how his readiness to "rescue" others also disposed him to set up family triangles that actually impeded the settling of differences between the original parties. He would not let this tendency, however, deter him from the volunteer work in the program. "I live with the tension. It's bear with it or shrivel up," he mused.

Louise, seventy-seven, had had to interrupt her participation in the program for open-heart surgery. Grateful for the extension of her health and without children of her own, she saw in the well-being of her foster grandchildren fruits of her own generativity. "I am doing something that matters, and I have a poem about it." With that she read from Alfred Lord Tennyson's *Ulysses:*

> *Old age hath yet his honour and his toil.*
> *Death closes all; but something ere the end,*
> *Some work of noble note, may yet be done,*
> *Not unbecoming men that strove with gods.*

Although there appeared to be nothing extraordinary in Louise's participation in the program, she knew that she was performing a "work of noble note," and was delighted.

Lorna, eighty-one, held similar sentiments. She found through her friendship with other adults in the program and through her ties with the children a warmth that she missed from her own children and grandchildren. "A lot of water has gone under that bridge," she said, dismissing references to her own family. The poem she chose, however, seemed to reveal the compensatory satisfaction the program offered her. She recited from Shelley's *To Mary . . . . . . .:*

> *Now has descended a serener hour,*
> *And with inconstant fortune, friends return;*
> *Though suffering leaves the knowledge and the power*
> *Which says: Let scorn be not repaid with scorn.*

The anxiety involved in trying to improve relationships with her own family would raise her discomfort enormously. This she knew. She chose, instead, the "serener hour" found in her relationships at school.

## Reminiscence

The incidence and content of reminiscence among older adults has also been a serious poetic theme. Many older adults find in the treatment of this theme an affirmation of their attention to the past. At a retirement community in New Jersey, the instructor for a continuing education course in creative writing provided multiple copies of anthologies of British and American poets. For their first assignment, the participants were to respond to any poem concerning reminiscence.

Francine began the next class session by reading from Shakespeare's *When to the Sessions of Sweet Silent Thought:*

> *When to the sessions of sweet silent thought*
> *I summoned up remembrance of things past,*
> *I sigh the lack of many a thing I sought,*
> *And with old woes new wail my dear time's waste;*
> *. . .*
> *And moan th' expense of many a vanished sight;*
> *Then can I grieve at grievances foregone,*
> *And heavily from woe to woe tell o'er*
> *The sad account of fore-bemoaned moan,*
> *Which I new pay as if not paid before.*

She had written at length about the pertinence of the poem to her own experience. She mentioned estranged relationships and failed goals that smarted in her memory as self-imposed and that continued to pain her now that she had endured their consequences.

Neighbors in attendance had heard Francine raise these points before. Mario spoke next. He introduced his remarks by saying that he "heard" the despondency which the sonnet echoed for Francine. He thought, however, that memory, when shared, contains its own relief, an opening to insight and self-acceptance. He preferred these lines from *The Prelude* by William Wordsworth:

> *How strange, that all*
> *The terrors, pains, and early miseries,*
> *Regrets, vexations, lassitudes interfused*
> *Within my mind, should e'er have borne a part,*
> *And that a needful part, in making up*

*The calm existence that is mine when I*
*Am worthy of myself!*

Mario insisted that memory is not merely neutral, but in service of renewal, of wholeness and healing.

Dorothy Ann sought the floor next. She had rummaged through the texts of poetry until Robert Southey's *Remembrance* struck her with the verse:

*Life's vain delusions are gone by;*
*Its idle hopes are o'er;*
*Yet Age remembers with a sigh*
*The days that are no more.*

She appreciated the manner in which it expressed an ambivalence inherent in reminiscence. She recognized that on occasion she felt twinges of nostalgia even for periods that had been filled with "delusions" and dead ends.

## Frailty

Older adults use poetic imagery to express their own experience of how it feels, of what it means, to be older. The following examples come from residents who were participating in an oral history project in a health-related facility. The interviewers had asked the participants the week before to identify a poetic image that corresponded with their experience of aging.

Florence spoke up first. She was a widow who retired from her realty career after she suffered a disabling stroke. She read from John Keats' *Ode to a Nightingale:*

*Fade far away, dissolve, and quite forget*
*What thou amongst the leaves hath never known,*
*The weariness, the fever, and the fret*
*Here, where men sit and hear each other groan;*
*Where palsy shakes a few, sad, last gray hairs,*

> *Where youth grows pale, and specter-thin, and dies;*
> *Where but to think is to be full of sorrow*
> *And leaden-eyed despairs,*
> *Where Beauty cannot keep her lustrous eyes,*
> *Or new Love pine at them beyond tomorrow.*

Each day challenged Florence to accept and enoble the chronic physical limitations that beset her in later years. The cadenced dignity Keats gave to this often wearisome task helped to sustain her resolve.

Rebecca had chosen a similarly somber poem that she favored for the "gentle twist" of its conclusion. She referred the interviewer to Shakespeare's *That Time of Year Thou Mayst in Me Behold*:

> *That time of year thou mayst in me behold*
> *When yellow leaves, or none, or few, do hang*
> *Upon those boughs which shake against the cold,*
> *Bare ruined choirs where late the sweet birds sang.*
> *In me thou see'st the twilight of such day*
> *As after sunset fadeth in the west,*
> *Which by and by black night doth take away,*
> *Death's second self, that seals up all the rest.*
> *In me thou see'st the glowing of such fire*
> *That on the ashes of his youth doth lie,*
> *As the death-bed whereon it must expire,*
> *Consumed with that which it was nourished by*
> *This thou perceiv'st, which makes thy love more strong,*
> *To love that well which thou must leave ere long.*

She did not deny she felt "consumed," but found therein an occasion for valuing the abilities and time left to her and for maintaining through audiotapes and correspondence the relationships that meant so much to her.

At this point, Gloria remarked that the preceding themes seemed to compose a "harmony" that ideally suffuses a person's later years with a quality of their own. She read from Shelley's *Hymn to Intellectual Beauty* to illustrate this "harmony:"

*The day becomes more solemn and serene*
*When noon is past—there is a harmony*
*In autumn, and a lustre in its sky,*
*Which through the summer is not heard or seen,*
*As if it could not be, as if it had not been!*
*Thus let thy power, which like the truth*
*Of nature on thy passive youth*
*Descended, to my onward life supply*
*Its calm—to one who worships thee,*
*And every form containing thee,*
*Whom, Spirit fair, thy spells did bind*
*To fear himself, and love all human kind.*

There is comfort, she clarified, in understanding that this harmony is a fruit of aging found only in its own season.

## Themes Concerning Family Systems

Many older adults who have appraised the dynamics of their own families have noticed the poetic themes and images about the influence of family history in members' lives. It is as though a poet's dramatic presentation of personal struggles had been drawn from observations of their own experiences. Those older adults, for example, who had participated in a mini-course on "Family History/Reminiscence" held at a neighborhood senior citizens center had an anthology of poetry included among their readings. Richard, in the fifth generation of sons bearing his name, had only recently recognized the life plan that he had spent a lifetime carrying out. When he came upon *The Flood* by Robert Frost, he recognized that the following lines about "blood" captured his new insights into his family's heritage:

*Just when we think we have it impounded safe*
*Behind new barrier walls (and let it chafe!),*
*It breaks away in some new kind of slaughter.*
*We choose to say it is let loose by the devil!*
*But power of blood itself releases blood.*

For Richard, "blood" epitomized the generations that transmitted the life plans of his family.

Ruth, a second participant, had chosen a poem that captured her own experience of cherishing a private world she had created to house so many unshared feelings of hurt. She came from a "reconstituted" family in which her mother had remarried a man with children of his own. Her mother and stepfather had each expected her to share their own animosity toward their first spouses, even to the point of discouraging her relationship with her deeply loved paternal grandparents. When she, in turn, had grandchildren, she felt that her sensitivity to cut-off relationships had led her to be overprotective of her grandchildren and overinvolved in her children's marriages. Robert Frost's *Revelation* expressed her own readiness to share with a confidant the anxiety from this toxic issue that she had kept to herself through these generations:

> *We make ourselves a place apart*
> *Behind light words that tease and flout,*
> *But oh, the agitated heart*
> *Till someone find us really out.*

For Ruth, the "agitated heart" represented the way she had internalized her own family's antagonisms. She was weary and angry at her inability to "start afresh" with the younger generations.

A third participant, Raymond, selected a poem which spoke to him of the ease with which toxic issues raise anxiety throughout households and across generations. He read from *The World Is Too Much With Us* by William Wordsworth:

> *The world is too much with us; late and soon*
> *Getting and spending, we lay waste our powers:*
> *Little we see in Nature that is ours;*
> *We have given our hearts away, a sordid boon!*

Raymond's insight from these lines was that his own personal boundaries had been so porous that he had dissipated his affections without thought about what ought to matter to him.

## Themes Concerning Providence

Older adults who are religiously motivated often look to poetry for images of God's providential guidance in their lives. Some rely upon explicitly religious images but many find in the symbols and metaphors of secular verse compelling witness to a divine companionship that they now recognize had managed "to write straight with the crooked lines" of their personal history.

At an ecumenically sponsored community center for older adults, a long established coterie of women had been discussing an anthology of English and American poets. Agnes spoke up first. She had discovered an expression of her own belief in William Wordsworth's *The Excursion: Despondency Corrected:*

> *One adequate support*
> *For the calamities of mortal life*
> *Exists—one only; an assured belief*
> *That the procession of our fate, howe'er*
> *Sad or disturbed, is ordered by a Being*
> *Of infinite benevolence and power;*
> *Whose everlasting purposes embrace*
> *All accidents, converting them to good.*

The group agreed that events "sad or disturbed" could, nonetheless, reveal God's caring presence and draw persons to achieve their potential.

Vera asked to read an excerpt from Edmund Waller's *Old Age* that continued the theme of God's fidelity. The losses and decrements that accompany aging, she suggested, are really opportunities for self-knowledge and self-fulfillment. God transforms limitations and weaknesses into graced occasions. She read:

> *The soul's dark cottage, battered and decayed,*
> *Lets in new light through chinks that Time hath made.*

Julie spoke up next, prefacing her selection with reminiscences about a compulsion to sabotage relationships with those who befriended her. She found God's presence in the anguishing consequences that finally moved her to examine and moderate her behavior. She addressed God with the words of John Donne's *Holy Sonnets, XIX:*

> *Batter my heart, for you*
> *As yet but knock; Breathe, shine, and seek to mend;*
> *That I may rise and stand, o'erthrow me and bend*
> *Your face, to break, blow, burn, and make me new.*

The violence of the images unsettled the group at first, but Lucia, the oldest member, identified with Julie's intensity. She believed that God's own spirit was within her as a resource she could draw upon when she was vulnerable. She expressed her relationship to God in the images of Shelley's *Ode to the West Wind:*

> *Oh, lift me as a wave, a leaf, a cloud!*
> *I fall upon the thorns of life! I bleed!*
> *A heavy weight of hours has chain'd and bow'd*
> *One too like thee: tameless, and swift, and proud.*

She so much enjoyed the idea that both God and she were "tameless" that she entertained her colleagues for the next hour with reminiscences about her resilience in the face of persons and events which would have broken the spirit of most others.

## Themes Concerning Death And Dying

Older adults find many images in poetry that express their own sentiments toward dying. The following examples of imagery were found in the journals and correspondence of older adults.

Alice was in her eighties when she died. She had been house-bound for seven years by then. She was without kin in this country and, with the exception of occasional visits to a clinic, had regular contact only with the Meals-On-Wheels volunteer. She did, however, maintain a daily journal that spanned fifty-seven years. On three occasions during her final eighteen months, she described her readiness to die. In the first entry, she included the lines from *We'll Go No More A-Roving* by Lord Byron:

> *For the sword outwears its sheath,*
> *And the soul wears out the breast,*
> *And the heart must pause to breathe,*
> *And love itself have rest.*

Following the text, she wrote that her "soul and mind" had exhausted their "instrument." After a lifetime of "sharing and receiving love," she longed for a "rest." In her second and third entries she again referred to these verses as an "authentic" expression of her own feelings.

Ann Margaret, an unmarried woman who had been a nurse, lived in an adult home in Maryland. Because she was the only family member who resided east of the Rocky Mountains, she had maintained an enduring correspondence with a niece. In one letter written five weeks before her death, she copied the lines from John Neihardt's *Let Me Live Out My Years* to illustrate her own stance toward dying:

> *And grant me, when I face the grisly Thing,*
> *One haughty cry to pierce the gray Perhaps!*
> *O let me be a tune-swept fiddlestring*
> *That feels the Master Melody—and snaps!*

She admitted to "a certain bellicosity" toward the prospect of dying which she hoped would not prevent her from some "final feeling of expansiveness."

Joel had chosen *Prospice* by Robert Browning because it presented his own stance toward death. He viewed his death as an event that dramatized the commonality, the shared experience, of human beings. He had lived according to the ethic that "we are all in this together," and he saw his death as confirming the significance of this conviction. He read:

> *I would hate that death bandaged my eyes, and forebore,*
> *And bade me creep past.*
> *No! let me taste the whole of it, fare like my peers*
> *The heroes of old,*
> *Bear the brunt, in a minute pay glad life's arrears*
> *Of pain, darkness, and cold.*

Poetry even seems to have abetted the unnoticed old age of seventy-nine-year-old Thomas, who died in a municipal shelter for the homeless. Among his possessions was a daily journal that logged the vagaries of his last seven years. There were cryptic philosophical snippets, addresses for food and shelter, and frequent humorous anecdotes about unpleasant encounters he had had in the course of the day. Scattered throughout were lines of poetry that he had copied in libraries, with occasional references to the lines' relevance to his own life. In an entry devoted to the theme of dying, Thomas noted his wry awareness of his ambivalence about dying and quoted from Pope's *The Dying Christian to His Soul* to illustrate his own experience:

> *Vital spark of heav'nly flame!*
> *Quit, oh quit this mortal frame;*
> *Trembling, hoping, ling'ring, flying,*
> *Oh the pain, the bliss of dying!*
> *Cease, fond Nature, cease thy strife,*
> *And let me languish into life.*

He concluded, several entries later, that he was "ready for something better than this time offered," and anticipated that upon dying he would find an improvement.

## Conclusion

Poetry is a readily accessible resource that prompts and enriches life review. Anthologies of British and American poetry are likely to contain some entries for every taste. Older adults can sample poems at their leisure, reflecting upon them privately or sharing the poems and the memories they evoke with a confidant or with a group organized for that purpose.

Many older adults find poetry replete with images that express the meaning of events and relationships that have surfaced in their life review. The beauty and dignity with which poems have portrayed the characteristics of older adults, especially the wisdom drawn from experiences of a lifetime, affirm older adults and their attention to life review. Poetic themes concerned with family relationships, with a providential and gracious meaning for one's life, and with dying are particularly evocative of personal content relevant to life review.

Poetry can enhance the humanistic, expansive dimension of life review. In this respect, it is similar to life review as a religious experience, the subject of the following chapter. Both poetry and faith can offer a perspective that finds in life review a panoply of reasons to conclude that the lives of older adults have been, and continue to be, worth living.

# 5

# Life Review as a Spiritual Experience

## Introduction

The preceding chapters have explored the psychological benefits of life review. This chapter explains how religiously committed older adults approach life review as a source of spiritual benefit, as well. Many of them describe their experiences of life review as graced moments that enrich their intimacy with a caring God. With this perspective they transform their life review from a developmental phenomenon enhancing "ego integrity" to a faith-filled, ongoing give-and-take exchange with God as confidant.

Religiously committed older adults tend to interpret their life review in terms of three themes. The first theme reappraises vulnerabilities arising from their own life plan as favored opportunities for God's caring involvement in their lives. The second theme emphasizes the trust that God will bring their unfinished lives and those of their descendants to personal fulfillment. The final theme portrays God as the Unconditional Lover who is companion to them throughout life and death.[1]

## Reappraising Personal Vulnerabilities

We have seen that when older adults review the trajectory of their lives, they eventually recall instances of repeated behavior that confirm the persistence of toxic issues and family triangles. Indeed, it would be easy for them to conclude that their life plan had more powerfully influenced their personal history than had any conviction or felt experience that God was drawing them to a fulfilling intimacy. Ironically, however, older believers tend to conclude that their life plan has been one of the more fruitful, if convoluted, avenues through which God has drawn good from their life history.

This does not deny, of course, the genuine pain of regret and guilt that accompanies memories of hurtful behavior. Yet, older adults do not tend to belabor the harm or waste that life review surveys. They prefer, rather, to see such episodes now as the grist for their present conversion. For example, at a party to celebrate the eightieth birthday of a family matriarch, the honoree identified "the tree of the knowledge of good and evil" with her "family tree," and interpreted "original sin" as a metaphor for the cumulative effect of the life plans and toxic issues that the adults had transmitted to their children. In response, her older brother, reflecting on the turbulent course of his own years, applied to himself the father's delight found at the conclusion of the parable of the Prodigal Son (Luke 15:20–24): "We had to celebrate and rejoice! *I* was dead and have come back to life. *I* was lost and am found."

Seventy-four-year-old Roseann was another older adult who viewed her life plan as an entry for God's own initiatives. She reported how her "relentless attention" to the comfort of her widowed mother had undermined her marriage and estranged her from her son. Although her family lived twenty miles from her mother's home, she had traveled there daily, more, she saw now, out of a fierce denial of her own needs than in response to requests from her mother. At day's end, she had little patience left for her husband's plans for their own family. She thrived, rather, on being indispensable to her mother and being "martyred" at home. When she eventually divorced, she sued her husband vindictively. Only her son's alienation, which cut her off from his children as well, finally alerted her to own mean spiritedness. In a local counseling agency she joined a psychotherapeutic group, and from the associations she made there, has spent the past eighteen years as a volunteer recruiting foster parents. She cited Ezekiel (34:15–16) to express her joy at the redirection of her life plan's compulsive outreach: "I myself will pasture my sheep. The lost I will seek out, the strayed I will bring back, the injured I will bind up, the sick I will heal." "As one of the lost, strayed, and injured," she continued, "I had first claim on the Lord's attention."

Those older adults who now recognize that God has been present to them throughout their life generally do not conclude that God has therein diminished their freedom. Rather, they convey that God's involvement appears tailored to the particulars of their life. An elderly shut-in, for example, described God's initiatives in her life in the words of Psalm 139: 5, 9–10: "Behind me and before, you hem me in and rest your hand upon me. If I take the wings of the dawn, if I settle at the farthest limits of the sea, even there your hand shall guide me and your right hand hold me fast." She saw these initiatives not as intrusive or constricting, but as caring gestures extending security and respite.

During a week-long retreat, Dan explained to his colleagues how his life review was an ongoing spiritual experience. Dan is a sixty-nine-year-old widower, a clinical psychologist recently retired from private practice and relocated from Delaware to the Southwest. He talked with his fellow retreatants about a dominant theme in his life—winning. Dan was descended from a line of "winners." He had been raised with stories of how his French immigrant grandfather won promotions from his mail-room position by a series of money-saving recommendations. He shared his memories of his mother in her fifties, arthritis notwithstanding, besting her siblings in fiercely contested games of handball. He recalled the faded parchments framed on their living room wall testifying to his parents' membership in ARISTA, their college honors society.

As a child, Dan had overheard his mother preening to neighbors about his grammar school I.Q. scores. He recalled his jealousy when his mother complimented a friend's performance in a high school play in which he also had a part, and his public challenge at his cousin's graduation that he would win ten medals when he graduated for the one awarded her that day. Indeed, he had graduated first in his class from high school, and won a scholarship to college.

Dan said that at college he espoused civil rights activities and a variety of social justice issues. He seriously weighed majoring in social work, with a goal toward a career that would involve him full time in the causes that mattered to him. He chose, instead, to major in psychology because of its greater prestige among careers in the human services.

Then he began to speak of his only child, a daughter. Dan remembered her tears as an adolescent whenever she lost to him at ping pong or chess. In her senior year of high school she resisted applying to any colleges but those in the Ivy League. When she was wait-listed among this eminent group, she salvaged her reputation with her peers by matriculating overseas at Cambridge. Then, during junior year she developed bulimia and had to withdraw from classes for a semester. She was separated from both those who had entered Cambridge with her and from her American friends at home. After her graduation, Dan seldom saw her. She settled in England and an intimacy never developed between them.

"So, where did 'winning' get me?" Dan compared himself to the seed that "fell among briars" (Luke 8:7 and 14), "And the thorns growing up with it stifled it. . . . The seed fallen among briars are those who hear, but their progress is stifled by the cares and riches and pleasures of life and they do not mature." He wryly noted that, together with his forebears, he and his daughter seem to have preferred the "cares" and discipline involved in "winning" even to "riches and pleasures." His grandparents' ambition for social mobility had set a family trajectory that he followed in turn, until its self-destructive course was evident in the skewing of his daughter's life.

Dan did not count their lives, however, as so much loss. The generations of discipline did fashion people ready to persevere in fields of human service for altruistic goals. Aware of the folly of the family's "winning ways," he hoped to mellow further, and model "a more caring style" for his daughter.

## Personal Fulfillment Is in God's Hands

Older adults confront the reality that ordinarily they will die unfinished—without having achieved their potential, without having provided restitution where justice required it, and without having blunted for their descendants the life plans that they have helped transmit. Life review, however, also has a forward cast to it that can engage older adults all the more actively with the persons and issues in their life.[2] Their reflections upon their own unresolved conflicts can lead them to creative insights for themselves, their peers, and younger people who may be caught up in the same conflicts. Ultimately, these older believers report that life review has shown them that fulfillment must be God's work, not their own.

To use the insights derived from life review in a manner constructive to relationships with adult children, grandchildren, or other kin is a heroic task. Older adults know they often have little influence among younger generations, and that their efforts to increase it may only aggravate problems. Memories of older relatives who interfered in their own lives give further pause. The wellbeing of future generations must ultimately be left to the same God who has accompanied them throughout life. One grandfather confided, "When I see my grandchildren living out my own failings, I reassure myself with the text [Jeremiah 29:11–13], 'I know well the plans I have in mind for you, . . . plans for your welfare, not for your woe! plans to give you a future full of hope. When you call me, I will listen to you. When you look for me, you will find me.' The issues in their lives are beyond my control. I have to entrust them to a caring God."

Russ is an example of an older adult who found God's presence in his life review. He is trying, in the modest ways still available to him, to draw upon that presence for the future. He is seventy-three years old, divorced, a recovered alcoholic who achieved sobriety while on parole from a prison sentence for attempted manslaughter. He maintains that the life review he began intermittently during his sentence precipitated his religious conversion, his outreach to his estranged daughter, and his participation in a self-help group for spouse abusers.

When Russ drank heavily, he regularly assaulted his wife. When he was sober, he was irritable and critical of her abilities as wife, mother, and housekeeper. To restrain his arbitrary and punitive conduct, his wife began to criticize their daughter's behavior in the hope that this would divert his attention. Within a few months, however, without even graduating from high school, their daughter married a man she barely knew. Russ paid no mind to his wife's accounts of their son-in-law's manhandling of their daughter. In fact, the two men eventually became drinking partners and business associates.

Russ's wife had long since divorced him. His daughter had married three drinking, brawling men in succession, and by her last husband had had a son. When Russ was released on parole, he did not even know where his daughter lived. Finding her and reaching out for reconciliation were the easy parts. Accepting his inability to modify her dysfunctional lifestyle was much harder. His mission for the future is to preserve his sobriety day by day, befriend his daughter and grandson, and continue his sponsorship of self-help groups of men who share his personal history. "This tough part isn't forever," he says. "You know,—God 'will wipe every tear from their eyes, and there will be no more death or mourning, crying out or pain, for the former world has passed away.' " (Revelation 21:4)

## God as Unconditional Lover

A spiritual counselor has summarized the relationship between older adults' perception of God as Unconditional Lover and the maintenance of their own self-esteem in these terms:

> . . . they know that in the Lord's creative and sustaining love for each of them, they *are* much more than they do, for what they do is necessarily limited by time and space, while who they are is rooted in the infinity of God's unique love for each of them.[3]

Indeed, by basing their self-worth upon God's unconditional love for them, these older adults have adopted a perspective radically different from a cultural appraisal that depreciates the value of those who suffer the physical and social losses that can accompany aging. From a spiritual perspective, those older adults, for instance, who are now without spouse and cherished companions, without accoutrements of prestige and power, without mobility and strength, or even without self-determination can affirm that their losses have no bearing upon their inherent self-worth.

Scenes from life review that reveal God as Unconditional Lover liberate many older adults from the image of a ledger-bearing God condemning people to punishment in this life and the next. Though their own lifestyle, values, and choices may have largely contributed to the losses and diminution that afflict them now, they are loved. Eighty-six-year-old Brigid, who never married and currently lives in a senior citizen apartment building, cited herself as a case in point. She was the sole survivor in her family from her generation and lived more than three hundred fifty miles from any relatives. Only recently she had begun a correspondence with a few nieces. Thirty years before, Brigid had alienated herself from her kin when a cousin was about to marry a black man, and her family was threatening to boycott the wedding en masse. When the cousin "defied" her kin, they stayed away and severed further contact with her. Before the wedding, Brigid voiced her dissent from the family's boycott in a searing, self-righteous diatribe. She had no regret about her dissent. That she would do again. It was her overweening claim of moral superiority that the family found so insufferable that they cut her off as well.

Brigid admitted her arrogance was a lifelong pattern that had frequently alienated others. When she was with associates, she tried to monitor herself. With kin, however, the prerogatives she had always held as the firstborn child aggravated her superciliousness and their sensitivity to it. Now she was trying to undo the past. She resolved to attend the next funeral in the family as a first step toward a reconciliation among all the parties. She knew she had to proceed patiently, absorbing the suspicions her initiatives would provoke. She knew too, she said, that "God's folly is wiser than men and his weakness more powerful than men." (1 Corinthians 1:25) She concluded that she had seen God's wisdom and power through the apertures of her own folly and weakness.

From a spiritual vantage point, the losses and diminutions surveyed in life review become "little deaths" that draw many older adults to seek self-fulfillment primarily in an intimate relationship with God. Finally, the prospect of death itself emphasizes that the goals presented in their life plan are illusory and out of reach. The comforting assurance of God's unconditional love eases abandonment to this same God in the face of death.

Ninety-two-year-old Natalie, lingering in a skilled nursing facility, whispered verses of Psalm 16, 5–6, 9–10, to convey this very point:

> O Lord, my allotted portion and my cup,
> you it is who hold fast my lot.
> For me the measuring lines have fallen on pleasant sites;
> . . .

Therefore my heart is glad and my soul rejoices,
my body, too, abides in confidence:
Because you will not abandon my soul to the nether world,
nor will you suffer your faithful one to undergo
      corruption.

This final abandonment to Providence can also fill older believers with confidence that after death they will be reunited with deceased family members and friends in full intimacy with God. Many refer to this prospect as fulfilling a deep need for resurrecting relationships that had been severed by misunderstanding, obduracy, and assorted family cutoffs even before death finalized the break. They await answers to so many questions. "Many adults say," for instance, "that they wished their parent had lived longer so they could have gotten a clearer picture of what that parent's feelings about them were because now it's rather hazy."[4] Some have surmised scenarios about the childhood and environmental conditions of grandparents and ancestors and look forward to learning how accurate their intuitions have been.

Lena's imminent death offers another relevant example. She was a hospice patient in the end stage of renal failure. She routinely asked visitors to join her in thanksgiving for God's fidelity in caring for her wellbeing throughout her life. She repeated for each visitor the convenant that God had kept toward her. "Hear me, . . . My burden since your birth, whom I have carried from your infancy. Even to your old age I am the same. Even when your hair is gray I will bear you. It is I who have done this, I who will continue, and I who will carry you to safety" (Isaiah 46:3–4). She chortled that God should have the gray hair after the kind of life she had led.

Lena could detail decades of alcoholism, ripoffs of kin, scams that netted her time in jail, and a string of sexual liaisons. Only in the last decade had she experienced a conversion, which led her to Alcoholics Anonymous. Alcoholics who relapsed found threads of hope in their relationship with her. Several visited her at the hospice, coming to say "goodbye," still with alcohol upon their breath.

She recalled with them their shared neediness, solicitude, and confrontations. Sober or drunk, she insisted they were all saved sinners. Vigorous or frail, they needed one another's company. She left them with the memory of her assurance that she will be awaiting them.

## Conclusion

Life review can be a spiritual experience concerned with the meaning of life and providing a foundation for self-acceptance and reconciliation. From a perspective of faith, life review elicits three themes for older adults: that personal vulnerabilities arising from life plans have also been favored opportunities for God's presence in their lives; that God will bring their "unfinished" lives and those of their descendants to personal fulfillment; that God is the "unconditional lover" who is companion throughout their lives and in their death.

# References

## Chapter 1

1. Lewis, C. 1971. Reminiscing and self-concept in old age. *Journal of Gerontology* 26(2):242.
2. Pincus, A. 1970. Reminiscence in aging and its implications for social work practice. *Social Work* (July). 50.
3. Rosengarten, T. 1979. Stepping over cockleburs: Conversations with Ned Cobb. In Pachter, M. (Ed.), *Telling lives: The biographer's art.* Washington, D.C.: New Republic Books. 117.
4. Cameron, P. 1972. The generation gap: Time orientation. *The Gerontologist* 12:117–119.
   Giambra, L. M. 1977. Daydreaming about the past: The time setting of spontaneous thought intrusions. *The Gerontologist* 17:35–38.
5. Merriam, S. 1980. The concept and function of reminiscence: A review of the research. *The Gerontologist* 20(5):604–609.
6. Clements, W. 1981. Reminiscence as the cure of souls in early old age. *Journal of Religion and Health* 20(1):41–47.
7. Jung, C. G. 1934. *Modern man in search of a soul.* New York: Harcourt, Brace, and Company.
8. Levinson, D. J. 1978. *The seasons of a man's life.* New York: Ballantine.
9. Lewis, C. 1973. The adaptive value of reminiscing in old age. *Journal of Geriatric Psychiatry* 6(1):117–121.
10. Ebersole, P. 1976. Reminiscing. *American Journal of Nursing* 76(8):1305.
11. Carlson, C. 1984. Reminiscing: Toward achieving ego integrity in old age. *Social Casework* (February). 86.
12. Revere, V., and S. Tobin. 1980–1981. Myth and reality: The older person's relationship to his past. *International Journal of Aging and Human Development* 12(1):15–25.
13. McMahon, A., and P. Rhudick. 1967. Reminiscing in the aged: An adaptational response. In Levin, S., and Kahana, R. (Eds.), *Psychody-*

*namic studies on aging: Creativity, reminiscing, and dying.* New York: International Universities Press.

14. Hughston, G., and S. Merriam. 1982. Reminiscence: A nonformal technique for improving cognitive functioning in the aged. *International Journal of Aging and Human Development* 15(2):139–149.

15. Cook, J. B. 1984. Reminiscing: how it can help confused nursing home residents. *Social Casework* (February). 92.

16. Coleman, P. G. 1974. Measuring reminiscence characteristics from conversation as adaptive features of old age. *International Journal of Aging and Human Development* 5(3):281–294.

17. Lewis, M., and R. Butler. 1974. Life-review therapy: Putting memories to work in individual and group psychotherapy. *Geriatrics* (November). 169. Reprinted with permission.

18. Butler, R. 1963. The life review: An interpretation of reminiscence in the aged. *Psychiatry* 26:70.

19. Ibid.

# Chapter 2

1. The following authors offer an insightful examination of "scripted" behavior from the perspective of Transactional Analysis:
Barnes, G. (Ed.) 1977. *Transactional analysis after Eric Berne.* New York: Harper's College Press. 214.
Berne, E. 1976. *Beyond Games and Scripts.* New York: Grove Press.
James, M. 1973. *Born to love.* Reading, MA: Addison-Wesley.
Steiner, C. 1971. *Games alcoholics play: The analysis of life scripts.* New York: Grove Press.
———. 1974. *Scripts people live.* New York: Grove Press.

2. Magee, J. 1988. The relevance of life review to the vowed life. *Review for Religious.* To be published. Reprinted with permission.

3. Fogarty, T. 1977. Fusion. *The Family* 4(2):56.

4. ———. 1975. Triangles. *The Family* 2(2):13.

5. The following authors present a clear analysis of these triangle positions from the perspective of Transactional Analysis:
James, M. 1975. *The ok boss.* Reading, MA: Addison-Wesley.
James, M., and D. Jongeward. 1975. The people book. Reading, MA: Addison-Wesley.
Jongeward, D., and M. James. 1973. *Winning with people.* Reading, MA: Addison-Wesley.

6. Fogarty, T. 1975. 14.

7. Magee, J. 1980. A family systems context for life script analysis. *Transactional Analysis Journal* 10(4):326–329.
8. Roman, M., and P. Raley. 1980. *The indelible family*. New York: Ransom, Wade. 182.
9. James, M. 1973. 137.
10. Price, D. 1980. Family constellation and projection process in personality development. *The Family* 7(2):78.
11. Markus, H. 1981. Sibling personalities: The luck of the draw. *Psychology Today* (June). 36.
12. Toman, W. 1969. *Family constellation: Its effect on personality and social behavior*. New York: Springer Publishing Company. 18.
13. Dell, P., and A. Appelbaum. 1977. Trigenerational enmeshment: Unresolved ties of single parents to family of origin. *American Journal of Orthopsychiatry* 47(1):56.

# Chapter 3

1. Lewis, M., and R. Butler. 1974. Life-review therapy: Putting memories to work in individual and group psychotherapy. *Geriatrics* (November). 169. Reprinted with permission.
2. Magee, J. 1987. Confidants help older religious with life review. *Review for Religious* 47(2):233–239. Reprinted with permission.
3. Kaminsky, M. 1978. Pictures from the past: The use of reminiscence in casework with the elderly. *Journal of Gerontological Social Work* 1(1):21.
4. Clements, W. M. 1979. *Care and counseling of the aging*. Philadelphia: Fortress Press. 60.
5. Wiebe, K. F. 1979. *Good times with old times: How to write your memoirs*. Scottdale, PA: Herald Press. 47.
6. Wakin, E. 1976. *Enter the Irish-American*. New York: Thomas Y. Crowell. 23.
7. LoGerfo, M. 1980–1981. Three ways of reminiscence in theory and practice. *International Journal of Aging and Human Development* 12(1):43.
8. Beesing, M., R. Nogosek. and P. O'Leary. 1984. *The enneagram*. Denville, NJ: Dimension Books. 171.
9. Wysocki, M. R. 1983. Life review for the elderly patient. *Nursing* 83:47–48.
10. Hateley, B. J. 1984. Spiritual well-being through life histories. *Journal of Religion and Aging* 1(2):65.
11. Simons, G. F. 1978. *Keeping your personal journal*. New York: Paulist Press. 71.

12. Progoff, I. 1977. *At a journal workshop: The basic text and guide for using the intensive journal process.* New York: Dialogue House. 173–174.

## Chapter 4

1. Magee, J. 1989. Using poetry as an aid to life review. *Activities, Adaptation, and Aging* 11(3). Reprinted with permission of Haworth Press, 12 West 32 Street, New York, NY.
"The Flood" is copyright 1928 by Holt, Rinehart and Winston, Inc. and renewed 1956 by Robert Frost. Reprinted from *The Poetry of Robert Frost*, edited by Edward Connery Lathem, by permission of Henry Holt and Company, Inc.
"Revelation" is copyright 1934 by Holt, Rinehart and Winston, Inc. and renewed 1962 by Robert Frost. Reprinted from *The Poetry of Robert Frost*, edited by Edward Connery Lathem, by permission of Henry Holt and Company, Inc.
"Let Me Live Out My Years," from *Lyric and Dramatic Poems*, by John G. Neihardt, published by the University of Nebraska Press, is reprinted with permission of the John G. Neihardt Trust.

### *Recommended Reading*

Allison, A. W. (Ed.) 1983. *The norton anthology of poetry.* 3rd ed. New York: W. W. Norton.

Baldwin, C., and H. G. Paul. (Eds.) 1985. *English Poems.* Great Neck, NY: Roth Publishers.

Campbell, J. T. (Ed.) 1983. *Our world's best loved poems.* Sacramento, CA: World Poetry Press.

Clark, T. C., and E. A. Gillespie (Eds.) 1979. *Quotable poems: An anthology of modern verse.* Darby, PA: Arden Library.

Friebert, S., and D. Young (Eds.) 1982. *Longman anthology of poetry: Contemporary American.* White Plains, NY: Longman Press.

Johnson, J. W. (Ed.) 1969. *The book of American negro poetry.* San Diego, CA: Harcourt, Brace, Jovanovich.

Nims, J. F. (Ed.) 1981. *The harper anthology of poetry.* New York: Harper and Row.

Williams, O. (Ed.) 1980. *Immortal poems of the English language.* New York: Washington Square Press.

# Chapter 5

1. Magee, J. Life review: A spiritual way for older adults. *Journal of Religion and Aging.* Vol. 3, No. 3/4, pp. 23–33, Spring/Summer 1987. Reprinted with permission of Haworth Press, 12 West 32 Street, New York, NY.
2. Bianchi, E. 1984. *Aging as a spiritual journey.* New York: Crossroads Publishing Company.
3. Caligiuri, A. 1979. Aging and the spiritual life. *Spiritual Life* 25(1):45.
4. Halpern, H. 1976. *Cutting loose: An adult guide to coming to terms with your parents.* New York: Simon and Schuster. 218.

# Bibliography

Adams, E. B. 1979. *Reminiscence and life review in the aged: A guide for the elderly, their families, friends, and service providers.* Denton, TX: North Texas State University.

Adams, V. 1981. The sibling bond: A lifelong love/hate dialectic. *Psychology Today* (June) 32–47.

Bank, S., and M. Kahn. 1982. *The sibling bond.* New York: Basic Books.

Barnes, G. (Ed.) 1977. *Transactional analysis after Eric Berne.* New York: Harper's College Press.

Baum, W. 1980–1981. Therapeutic value of oral history. *International Journal of Aging and Human Development* 12(1):49–53.

Becker, A. 1986. *Ministry with the older person: A guide for clergy and congregations.* Minneapolis: Augsburg.

Beesing, M., R. Nogosek and P. O'Leary. 1984. *The enneagram.* Denville, NJ: Dimension Books.

Berne, E. 1976. *Beyond Games and Scripts.* New York: Grove Press.

Bertaux, D. (Ed.) 1981. *Biography and society: The life history approach in the social sciences.* Beverly Hills: Sage Publications.

Bianchi, E. 1984. *Aging as a spiritual journey.* New York: Crossroads Publishing Company.

Bloomfield, H. 1983. *Making peace with your parents.* New York: Ballantine Books.

Blythe, R. 1979. *The view in winter: Reflections on old age.* New York: Harcourt, Brace, Jovanovich.

Boylin, W., S. Gordon, and M. Merle. 1976. Reminiscing and ego integrity in institutionalized elderly males. *Gerontologist* 16(2):118–124.

Brown, R., and J. Kulik. 1977. Flashbulb memories. *Cognition* 5:73–99.

Butler, R. 1971. Age: The life review. *Psychology Today* (December). 49–51, 89.

————. 1963. The life review: An interpretation of reminiscence in the aged. *Psychiatry* 26:65–76.

————. 1980–1981. The life review: An unrecognized bonanza. *International Journal of Aging and Human Development* 12(1):35–38.

————. 1974. Successful aging and the role of life review. *The Journal of the American Geriatric Society.* 22(12):529–535.

Carlson, C. 1984. Reminiscing: Toward achieving ego integrity in old age. *Social Casework* (February). 81–89.

Cameron, P. 1972. The generation gap: Time orientation. *Gerontologist* 12:117–119.

Carter, E., and M. McGoldrick (Eds.) 1980. *The family life cycle: A framework for family therapy.* New York: Gardner Press.

Cashman, E. 1986. *Facilitating the art of reminiscence.* Cincinnati: National Association of Church Personnel Administrators.

Castelnuovo-Tedesco, P. 1978. The mind as a stage: Some comments on reminiscence and internal objects. *International Journal of Psychoanalysis* 59:19–25.

Chubon, S. 1980. A novel approach to the process of life review. *Journal of Gerontological Nursing* 6(9):543–546.

Clements, W. M. 1979. *Care and counseling of the aging.* Philadelphia: Fortress Press.

Clements, W. 1981. Reminiscence as the cure of souls in early old age. *Journal of Religion and Health* 20(1):41–47.

Coleman, P. G. 1986. *Ageing and reminiscence processes.* New York: John Wiley and Sons.

————. 1974. Measuring reminiscence characteristics from conversation as adaptive features of old age. *International Journal of Aging and Human Development* 5(3):281–294.

Cook, J. B. 1984. Reminiscing: How it can help confused nursing home residents. *Social Casework* (February). 90–93.

Cooper, W. 1974. *Families: A memoir and a celebration.* New York: Harper and Row.

Costa, P., and R. Kastenbaum. 1967. Some aspects of memories and ambitions in centenarians. *The Journal of Genetic Psychology* 110:3–16.

David, D. 1981. *The uses of memory: Social aspects of reminiscence in old age.* Dissertation. Berkeley: University of California.

Davis, C., K. Back, and K. MacLean. 1977. *Oral history: From tape to type.* Chicago: American Library Association.

Dell, P., and A. Appelbaum. 1977. Trigenerational enmeshment: Unresolved ties of single-parents to family of origin. *American Journal of Orthopsychiatry* 47(1):52–59.

Demotts, J. 1981. *Reminiscence in older persons as a functionn of the cognitive control principle.* Dissertation. San Diego: California School of Professional Psychology.

de Ramon, P. 1983. The final task: life review for the dying patient. *Nursing* 83:46–49.

Dixon, J. 1977. *Preserving your past: A painless guide to writing your autobiography and family history.* Garden City, NY: Doubleday.

Dylong, J. 1979. *Living history 1925–1950: Family experiences of times remembered.* Chicago: Loyola University Press.

Ebersole, P. 1976. Reminiscing. *American Journal of Nursing* 76(8):1304–1305.

――――. 1976. Reminiscing and group psychotherapy with the aged. In Burnside, I.M. (Ed.), *Nursing and the aged.* New York: McGraw-Hill. 214–230.

Ellison, K. 1981. Working with the elderly in a life review group. *Journal of Gerontological Nursing* 7(9):537–541.

Emlet, C. 1979. Reminiscence: A psychosocial approach to institutionalized aged. *American Health Care Association Journal* 5(5):19–22.

Fairchild, R. 1978. *Lifestory conversations:* New dimensions in a ministry of evangelistic calling. New York: The United Presbyterian Church in the USA.

Fallot, R. 1979–1980. Impact on mood of verbal reminiscing in later adulthood. *International Journal of Aging and Human Development* 10(4):385–400.

Ferguson, J. 1980. *Reminiscence counseling to increase psychological well-being of elderly women in nursing home facilities.* Dissertation. Columbia: University of South Carolina.

Fischer, K. 1985. *Winter grace.* New York: Paulist Press.

Fishel, E. 1985. *Sisters: Love and rivalry inside the family and beyond.* New York: William Morrow.

Fogarty, T. 1977. Fusion. *The Family* 4(2):49–58.

――――. 1975. Triangles. *The Family* 2(2):11–19.

Framo, J. 1976. Family of origin as a therapeutic resource for adults in marital and family therapy: You can and should go home again. *Family Process* 15(2):193–210.

Georgemiller, R. 1982. *Life review therapy with older adults.* Dissertation. Pasadena, CA: Fuller Theological Seminary.

Giambra, L. M. 1977. Daydreaming about the past: The time setting of spontaneous thought intrusions. *Gerontologist* 17(1):35–38.

――――. 1974. Daydreaming across the lifespan: Late adolescence to senior citizen. *International Journal of Aging and Human Development* 5(2):115–140.

————. 1977. A factor analytic study of daydreaming, imaginal process and temperament: A replication on an adult male life-span sample. *Journal of Gerontology* 32(6):675–680.

Gluck, S. 1979. What's so special about women? Women's oral history. *Frontiers* 2(2):3–14.

Gorney, J. 1968. *Experiencing and aging: Patterns of reminiscence among the elderly.* Dissertation. Chicago: University of Chicago.

Hala, M. 1975. Reminiscence group therapy project. *Journal of Gerontological Nursing* 1(3):35–41.

Halpern, H. 1976. *Cutting loose: An adult guide to coming to terms with your parents.* New York: Simon and Schuster.

Harris, R., and S. Harris. 1980. Therapeutic uses of oral history techniques in medicine. *International Journal of Aging and Human Development* 12(1):27–33.

Hassel, D. 1977. Prayer of personal reminiscence: Sharing one's memories with Christ. *Review for Religious* 36(2):213–226.

Hasselkus, B. 1982. Use of monthly newsletter for life review: Case illustration. *Physical and Occupational Therapy in Geriatrics* 2(1):53–55.

Hateley, B. J. 1984. Spiritual well-being through life histories. *Journal of Religion and Aging* 1(2):63–71.

Hausman, C. 1980. Life Review Therapy. *Journal of Gerontological Social Work* 3(2):31–37.

Havighurst, R., and R. Glasser. 1972. Exploratory study of reminiscence. *Journal of Gerontology* 27(2):245–253.

Hiltner, S. (Ed.). 1975. *Toward a theology of aging.* New York: Human Sciences Press.

Holloway, W. 1977. Transactional analysis: An integrative view. In Barnes, G. (Ed.), *Transactional analysis after Eric Berne.* New York: Harper's College Press. 169–222.

Hughston, G., and S. Merriam. 1982. Reminiscence: A nonformal technique for improving cognitive functioning in the aged. *International Journal of Aging and Human Development* 15(2):139–149.

Hunter, W. W. 1953. *Older people tell their story.* Ann Arbor: University of Michigan Press.

Ingersoll, B., and L. Goodman. 1980. History comes alive: Facilitating reminiscence in a group of institutionalized elderly. *Journal of Gerontological Social Work* 2(4):305–319.

James, M. 1973. *Born to love.* Reading, MA: Addison-Wesley.

————. 1975. *The ok boss.* Reading, MA: Addison-Wesley.

James, M., and D. Jongeward. 1975. *The people book: Transactional analysis for students.* Reading, MA: Addison-Wesley.

James, M., and L. Savary. 1976. *The heart of friendship*. New York: Harper and Row.

Jenkins, S. 1978. *Past/present: Recording life stories of older people*. Washington, D.C.: St. Alban's Parish.

Jongeward, D., and M. James. 1973. *Winning with people*. Reading, MA: Addison-Wesley.

Jourard, S. M. 1959. Healthy personality and self-disclosure. *Mental Hygiene* 43(4):499–507.

Jung, C. G. 1933. *Modern man in search of a soul*. New York: Harcourt, Brace, and Company.

Kaminsky, M. 1978. Pictures from the past: The use of reminiscence in casework with the elderly. *Journal of Gerontological Social Work* 1(1):19–31.

———. (Ed.) 1984. *The uses of reminiscence: New ways of working with older adults*. New York: Haworth Press.

Kaufman, S. 1981. Cultural components of identity in old age: A case study. *Ethos* 9(1):51–87.

Keen, S., and A. Fox. 1973. *Telling your story: A guide to who you are and who you can be*. New York: The New American Library.

Kiernat, J. 1979. The use of life review activity with confused nursing home residents. *American Journal of Occupational Therapy* 33(5):306–310.

Kramer, C., J. Kramer, and H. Dunlop. 1966. Resolving grief. *Geriatric Nursing* (July-August). 14–17.

LeFevre, C., and P. LeFevre (Eds.) 1981. *Aging and the human spirit: A reader in religion and aging*. Chicago: Exploration Press.

Lesser, J., L. Lazarus, and S. Havasy. 1981. Reminiscence group therapy with psychotic geriatric inpatients. *Gerontologist* 21(3):291–296.

Levin, S., and R. Kahana (Eds.) 1967. *Psychodynamic studies on aging: Creativity, reminiscing, and dying*. New York: International Universities Press.

Levinson, D. J. 1978. *The seasons of a man's life*. New York: Ballantine.

Lewis, C. 1973. The adaptive value of reminiscing in old age. *Journal of Geriatric Psychiatry* 6(1):117–121.

———. 1971. Reminiscing and self-concept in old age. *Journal of Gerontology* 26(2):240–243.

Lewis, M., and R. Butler. 1974. Life-review therapy: Putting memories to work in individual and group psychotherapy. *Geriatrics* (November). 165–172.

Lichtman, A. J. 1978. *Your family history*. New York: Vintage Books.

Lieberman, M., and J. Flak. 1971. The remembered past as a source of data for research on the life cycle. *Human Development* 14:132–141.

Linn, M., and D. Linn. 1978. *Healing life's hurts: Healing memories through five stages of forgiveness*. New York: Paulist Press.

———. 1974. *Healing of memories*. New York: Paulist Press.

Liton, J., and S. Olstein. 1969. Therapeutic aspects of reminiscence. *Social Casework* 50:263–268.

LoGerfo, M. 1980–1981. Three ways of reminiscence in theory and practice. *International Journal of Aging and Human Development* 12(1):39–48.

McMahon, A., and P. Rhudick, 1964. Reminiscing: Adaptational significance in the aged. *Archives of General Psychiatry* 10:292–298.

———. 1967. Reminiscing in the aged: An adaptational response. In Levin, S., and Kahana, R. (Eds.), *Psychodynamic studies on aging: Creativity, reminiscing, and dying.* New York: International Universities Press. 64–78.

McKinley-Runyan, W. 1982. *Life histories and psychobiography.* New York: Oxford University Press.

Magee, J. 1987. Confidants help older religious with life review. *Review for Religious* 47(2):233–239.

———. 1980. A family systems context for life script analysis. *Transactional Analysis Journal* 10(4):326–329.

———. 1988. The relevance of life review to the vowed life. *Review for Religious.* To be published.

———. Life review: A spiritual way for older adults. *Journal of Religion and Aging.* Vol. 3, No. 3/4, pp. 23–33, Spring/Summer 1987.

———. 1989. Using poetry as an aid to life review. *Activities, Adaptation, and Aging* 11(3). To be published.

Markus, H. 1981. Sibling personalities: The luck of the draw. *Psychology Today* (June). 35–37.

Merriam, S. 1980. The concept and function of reminiscence: A review of the research. *Gerontologist* 20(5):604–609.

Morycz, R. 1980. Formative perspectives on life review and pastoral counseling for the elderly. *Studies in Formative Spirituality* 1(3):379–392.

Moriwaki, S. Y. 1973. Self-disclosure, significant others and psychological well-being in old age. *Journal of Health and Social Behavior* 14:226–232.

Myerhoff, B. 1980. Telling one's story. *The Center Magazine* 13(2):22–40.

Myerhoff, B., and A. Simic. 1978. *Life's career-aging.* Beverly Hills: Sage Publications.

Myerhoff, B., and V. Tufte. 1975. Life history as integration: An essay on an experimental model. *Gerontologist* 15:541–543.

Neisser, U. (Ed.) 1982. *Memory observed: Remembering in natural contexts.* San Francisco: W. H. Freeman.

Nouwen, H., and W. Gaffney. 1974. *Aging.* Garden City, NY: Doubleday.

Parlade, R. 1982. *Reminiscence and problem solving approaches: A comparison study with a geriatric population.* Dissertation. Athens: University of Georgia.

Perrotta, P., and J. Meacham. 1981–1982. Can a reminiscing intervention alter depression and self-esteem? *International Journal of Aging and Human Development* 14(1):23–29.

Perschbacher, R. 1984. An application of reminiscence in an activity setting. *Gerontologist* 24(4):343–345.

Pincus, A. 1970. Reminiscence in aging and its implications for social work practice. *Social Work* (July). 47–53.

Pincus, L., and C. Dare. 1978. *Secrets in the family.* New York: Pantheon Books.

Price, C. 1983. Heritage: A program design for reminiscence. *Activities, Adaptation and Aging* 3(3):47–52.

Price, D. 1980. Family constellation and projection process in personality development. *The Family* 7(2):76–82.

Progoff, I. 1977. *At a journal workshop: The basic text and guide for using the intensive journal process.* New York: Dialogue House.

Revere, V., and S. Tobin. 1980–1981. Myth and reality: The older person's relationship to his past. *International Journal of Aging and Human Development* 12(1):15–25.

Roman, M., and P. Raley. 1980. *The indelible family.* New York: Ransom, Wade.

Romaniuk, M. 1983. The application of reminiscing to the clinical interview. *Clinical Gerontologist* 1(3):39–43.

———. 1981. Reminiscence and the second half of life. *Experimental Aging Research* 7(3):315–335.

Romaniuk, M., and J. G. Romaniuk. 1982–1983. Life events and reminiscence: A comparison of young and old adults. *Imagination, Cognition, and Personality* 2:125–136.

———. 1981. Looking back: An analysis of reminiscence functions and triggers. *Experimental Aging Research* 7(4):477–489.

Rosengarten, T. 1979. Stepping over cockleburs: Conversations with Ned Cobb. In Pachter, M. (Ed.), *Telling lives: The biographer's art.* Washington, D.C.: New Republic Books. 104–131.

Ryant, C. 1981. Comment: Oral history and gerontology. *Gerontologist* 21(1):104–105.

Ryden, M. 1981. Nursing intervention in support of reminiscence. *Journal of Gerontological Nursing* 7(8):461–463.

Sandell, S. 1978. Reminiscence and movement therapy with the aged. *Art Psychotherapy* 5(4):217–221.

Schmidt, M. 1975. Interviewing the "old old." *Gerontologist* (December). 544–547.

Shumway, G. L., and W. G. Hartley. 1974. *An oral history primer.* Salt Lake City: Deseret Books.

Shute, G. 1986. Life review: A cautionary note. *Clinical Gerontologist* 6(1):57–58.

Simons, G. F. 1978. *Keeping your personal journal.* New York: Paulist Press.

Smith, T. 1981. *In favor of growing older*. Scottdale, PA: Herald Press.

Sperbeck, D. 1982. *Age and personality effects on autobiographical memory in adulthood*. Dissertation. Rochester, NY: University of Rochester.

Spero, M. 1981–1982. Confronting death and the concept of life review: The Talmudic approach. *Omega* 12(1):37–43.

————. 1980. Death and the "life review" in halakhah. *Journal of Religion and Health* 19(4):313–319.

Steiner, C. 1971. *Games alcoholics play: The analysis of life scripts*. New York: Grove Press.

————. 1974. *Scripts people live*. New York: Grove Press.

Stringfellow, W. 1981. Biography as theology. *Katallagete* 7(4):36–39.

Studzinski, R. 1985. *Spiritual direction and midlife development*. Chicago: Loyola University Press.

Sullivan, C. 1982. Life review: A functional view of reminiscence. *Physical and Occupational Therapy in Geriatrics* 2(1):39–52.

Tekavec, C. 1982. *Self-actualization, reminiscence, and life satisfaction*. Dissertation. San Diego: California School of Professional Psychology.

Thompson, P. 1978. *The voice of the past: Oral history*. Oxford: Oxford University Press.

Thorson, J. A., and T. C. Cook (Eds.) 1980. *Spiritual well-being of the elderly*. Springfield, IL: Charles C. Thomas.

Tobin, S., and E. Etigson. 1968. Effect of stress on earliest memory. *Archives of General Psychiatry* 19(4):435–444.

Toman, W. 1969. *Family constellation: Its effect on personality and social behavior*. New York: Springer Publishing Company.

Watson, L. C. 1976. Understanding a life history as a subjective document. *Ethos* 4:95–131.

Watts, J., and A. Davis. 1978. *Generations: Your family in modern American history*. New York: Alfred Knopf.

Wiebe, K. F. 1979. *Good times with old times: How to write your memoirs*. Scottdale, PA: Herald Press.

Wrye, H., and J. Churilla. 1977. Looking inward, looking backward: Reminiscence and the life review. *Frontiers* 2(2):98–105.

Wysocki, M. R. 1983. Life review for the elderly patient. *Nursing* 83:47–48.

Zeiger, B. 1976. Life review in art therapy with the aged. *American Journal of Art Therapy* 15:47–50.

Zeitlin, S., et al. (Eds.) 1976. *Family Folklore*. Washington, D.C.: Smithsonian Institution.

# Index

# About the Author

D R. JAMES JOSEPH MAGEE is an associate professor of gerontology in the graduate school of the College of New Rochelle. He began his research into the life satisfaction of older adults after a practice in family therapy as a clinical social worker. He is the author of more than twenty articles, primarily devoted to life review, life satisfaction, and spirituality among older adults, and is a consultant to organizations sponsoring programs to enhance the life satisfaction of their retired members.